Dorris Blough Mur

W9-AOC-823

JOURNEY INTO THE LIGHT

Lessons of Pain and Joy
to Renew Your Energy and
Strengthen Your Faith

A SPECTRUM BOOK

Prentice-Hall, Inc., Englewood Cliffs, New Jersey 07632

Library of Congress Cataloging in Publication Data

Murdock, Dorris Blough.
    Journey into the light.

    (Steeple books)
    "A Spectrum Book."
    Includes index.
    1. Christian life — Church of the Brethren authors.
2. Consolation.   3. Murdock, Dorris Blough.   I. Title.
II. Series.
BV4501.2.M777 1984   248.4'8973   83-21312
ISBN 0-13-511460-8
ISBN 0-13-511452-7 (pbk.)

*Dedicated to my children and those caring friends
who reached out in my Darkness
and helped turn it into Light.*

10   9   8   7   6   5   4   3   2   1

ISBN 0-13-511460-8

ISBN 0-13-511452-7 {PBK.}

Editorial/production supervision by William P. O'Hearn
Cover design by Hal Siegel
Manufacturing buyer: Edward J. Ellis

This book is available at a special discount when ordered in
bulk quantities. Contact Prentice-Hall, Inc., General
Publishing Division, Special Sales, Englewood Cliffs, N.J. 07632.

Prentice-Hall International, Inc., *London*
Prentice-Hall of Australia Pty. Limited, *Sydney*
Prentice-Hall Canada Inc., *Toronto*
Prentice-Hall of India Private Limited, *New Delhi*
Prentice-Hall of Japan, Inc., *Tokyo*
Prentice-Hall of Southeast Asia Pte. Ltd., *Singapore*
Whitehall Books Limited, *Wellington, New Zealand*
Editora Prentice-Hall do Brasil Ltda., *Rio de Janeiro*

Contents

Preface

Each of us is walking through our own particular Darkness. Sometimes it is Darkness that we painted for ourselves; at other times it seems to come from the world outside, thrust upon us.

We long for patches of sunshine to warm our spirits and give us hope. We must learn that there are ways to create our own Light in the midst of Darkness. That is what this book is about. We can find warmth and light and renewed energy through faith. We find these things not through finding a God of magic, but by discovering how to be content at the very moment the Darkness is swirling around our heads. Such knowledge is the Secret of the Ages, known to every generation, and yet it must be relearned over and over.

Walter Brueggemann, contemporary theologian, says we are caught forever between the promises and the fulfillment in the darkness. But it is in the darkness that we meet God.[1]

When a child cries out in the night, Mother goes to the child and says three things:

"Don't be afraid."

"I'm here."

"Drink this."

When a child of God cries in the night, Father and Mother God comes to our side and says, "Be not afraid, for I am with you. The water that I give is living water."

We are all in the Darkness, the Darkness that separates us from one another and from God. But the mission of each of us is to reach out to those in darkness and say, "Don't be afraid; I'm here; drink this," which also says, "Don't be afraid; God is here; eat and drink of Him and you shall know peace."

The Twenty-third Psalm is a microcosm of our lives. It begins with the Promises: "The Lord is my shepherd; I shall not want; He maketh me to lie down in green pastures; He leadeth me beside the still waters; He restoreth my soul."

What promises!

Beauty, plenty, and peace of mind.

Then why don't we have those qualities of a happy life? Is it because in actuality we are forever in the Darkness?

"Yea, though I walk through the Valley of the Shadow of Death . . ." The fear of death, the threat of non-being, is paralyzing.

Each day of our lives we are in the Valley of the Shadow, in the Darkness, with the pain of being human and all the frailties to which we are heir.

Illness, loss, fear, hunger, pain, death—we experience them constantly. Look around you . . . see the pain written in faces and expressed in body language. Ask the question "How are things going for you?" and hear the cries of anguish rising from hearts scared of the dark.

Without question the most devastating problem is the breakdown in relationships between ourselves and the other people in our lives. Often we do not realize that the real cause is a breakdown in the relationship between ourselves and the God in our lives.

Our lives and our world are constantly being altered, particularly our relationships. We talk about wishing for certain things to happen in our lives—a new job, a new friend, a new marriage—but in actuality, change is frightening. Even a vacation trip is a change that often ends in disharmony and unpleasantness.

If, in the Darkness, we want to do something about our situation, we may be reluctant to make a change, for even the pain in which we find ourselves is still familiar pain. And *un*familiar pain could be worse, couldn't it?

Meeting God in the Darkness is the beginning of change, of transformation, unless we deny God access into our innermost selves.

It is the Transformation that concerns us in this book, the transformation from tired, fearful people to persons full of hope and energy.

Since transformation is ever a process of evolving, of discovering bits and pieces about ourselves, there are ways to minimize the damage we do to ourselves . . . and others . . . and to maximize the benefits, the growth that is possible. No one can cause transformation to happen in another person, but neither can someone keep it from happening.

Four years ago I entered the process of Transformation, although I was not aware that anything different was under way. In fact, I do not know the moment of the first faltering step. Only later did I realize what had happened, and that I was irrevocably on the way to a new level of understanding, to new heights of joy . . . and pain.

I discovered that "God loves me, and if God loves me, I'm worth loving. If I'm worth loving, I'm worth having a loving relationship with my husband." And I began to look for ways to bring that about. My counselor spoke of my transformation in psychological terms, of coming to love myself, to know myself as a person of worth, but I prefer the theological way of speaking.

I would not have said that I did not know God loves me, but in all of us there are compartments, parts of us that are not free. In relation to my husband, I was still in bondage, not to him, but to my fear of changing the relationship. When our four children were all out of the home, I wanted to begin to use some of my other talents which had been kept on the back burner all those years. As is true of so many couples married in the 1940s, any change in the relationship is upsetting; my husband was threatened by my wanting to achieve something he viewed as being outside the marriage. When we began to examine the relationship, the result was a divorce.

Divorce is only one of the life accidents that people find on their calendar in this time of social upheaval. The methods of coping with divorce are, in many ways, no different from those for most other life accidents. Over and over, meeting God in the Darkness is a similar experience, whether it is loss of job, loss of love, failure of some kind, loss of financial security, loss of a marriage, or loss of health.

As I entered the Darkness, all around me I became aware of other people also stumbling along, frightened, angry, bitter, lonely. Fortunately I had a number of people who said to me, "It's all right; don't be afraid; I'm here." In particular, there were three women who put themselves on twenty-four-hour call for six months while I was wandering, half-blind, in the gray mists.

Through a determination to come out of this with my integrity still intact, and with the help of some wise and caring people, I have discovered renewed energy through renewed faith.

My *Journey into the Light* is not ended; in fact, it will never really end, but over and over, people have said to me, "Write that down; that could be helpful to other people in similar experiences."

And so, these are the Lessons I have learned. This is not intended to be an exhaustive treatise. When your soul is open to the world around you, you catch glimpses of truth in many and strange places. Bits of understanding came from such varied sources as a snatch of a song, a line from a play, a comic strip, a sermon, a chance remark by a friend, but most of all, from the Bible. I trust that in these pages you may stumble upon a concept that you need and are ready for at that moment, and with an "Ah, hah!" you will put it to work in your life.

What has happened to me is not different, except perhaps in the ways I have found to express it. Brueggemann talks of "the power of words to create an alternative model."[2]

I have learned to "share the gift of pain," to spend time in my "desert," to "celebrate" beginnings and endings of my life, to recognize the "*shetan,*" the power for good or evil that lies within us, in myself. I want to share these concepts with you in the hope that words will have power to create an alternative model of faith in your life, a model of renewed hope and energy.

chapter one

The Gift of Pain

One of life's accidents has found you. You have lost something very precious, something vital to your well-being—your money, your job, your friend, your marriage.

How do you face the world and admit you failed? More difficult than that, how do you face your closest friends and admit you failed? But toughest of all, how do you face God? ". . . from whom no secrets are hid." He was the one you promised to be faithful to, and look what happened! And when are you ever going to quit feeling as if there were lead weights on your heart and your feet?

With the "world," you can pretend, put on a smiling face. But not so with friends. If you try to hide it, they will sense something is wrong and assume you do not want to share a very important part of your life with them. Or they will learn it from someone else, and that puts the friendship in jeopardy. (It is hardly safe to assume that "No one knows.")

This lesson came through a close friend who called one day to ask if it would be all right for her to come by later that afternoon. Although she tried to sound nonchalant, an undertone in her voice told me that something serious was in the air, and we set an appointment time.

When I opened the door, the look on her face told me that this friend needed to be held. I wrapped her in my arms and held her while she sobbed on my shoulder. When her tears eased, we sat down. She told me she had just learned that her sixteen-year-old daughter was pregnant. We talked a long time, discussing the various alternatives.

Then she said to me, "I wanted to come and tell you before you heard it from someone else."

"But, Janet," I said, "how difficult for you!"

"Yes, and no," she replied. "I could not hide such painful news from my best friend. Wherever I would have met you, at church, in the grocery store, I would have burst into tears. So, in a way, I was making it easier on myself."

"But you could have pretended that nothing had happened," I said, "and bluffed your way through this. If your daughter marries, if she decides to not keep the child, or to go away to have it, you could get by without telling anyone. And besides, you took a chance on being hurt because you made yourself vulnerable by admitting this. How did you know I wouldn't blame you or give you a sermon?"

"I thought about that," my friend said. "But I did what I had to do; share my pain with you because you are my friend."

"You have given me a gift," I said, "the gift of your pain, and I have a gift for you." I went to her then and hugged her again as I said, "Don't forget, I love you, and I will be here whenever you need me."

When she shared her pain, she gave me a gift, and I gave a gift in return, the gift of caring.

Remember David and Jonathan's love for each other that lasted a lifetime. When David had to flee for his life, "they kissed one another and wept with one another," for it was said of Jonathan

He loved David as he loved his own soul.

I SAMUEL 20:17 and 41

I have had occasion to use the lesson I learned from Janet, to share my pain; and I have realized that I shared it not for my friends, but for me. I thought I had shared to safeguard our friendship, but it was out of my *own* need that I found the courage (or the desperation) to share my pain.

With much reluctance I approached those friends, one by one. But my fear of going through the Darkness alone was greater than my fear of their recriminations.

Mark 4:24 described this: "The measure you give will be the measure you get, and still more will be given you," because there was another plus; the relationships moved to a higher level, for we had shared something deeply human. My friends had reached out to me in my Darkness and said, "It's all right; I'm here; don't be afraid." But even to this day, it is easier to give the gift of pain than to accept the caring in return, for it is difficult for us to accept any gift, especially emotional ones.

God is Love, and I felt that Love as it flowed through my friends and then into myself. From it I gained the strength to do my tasks during that time of crisis. Otherwise, I would have been incapacitated, immobilized with pain and fear, my energy dissipating itself in phony explanations and efforts to avoid talking about my situation.

When a life accident happens, one that involves a sense of failure on our part, the first tendency is to not let the world know we are hurting. If we hide our pain, we think, they won't know about it, and it will hurt less. Instead, it hurts more, for we have added fear to our pain, fear that they will find out anyway, and we will still have to admit our inadequacy.

Divorce is a public proclamation of failure, failure to do what you set out to do—have a good marriage. It doesn't matter what the cause is; there will be guilt feelings and a sense of failure.

Losing your job or an investment, or standing by while your child does any of a number of painful things also proclaims to the world that you were not as good as you should have been.

3

That is what you feel deep down in your gut. All are losses of a part of yourself, and the result is pain, wounds to the spirit, and oftentimes to the pocketbook as well.

We tend to believe that we are the only person who has done such a dumb thing, or who has sustained such a reprehensible loss, as the Psalmist who said, "I am a worm; all who see me mock me; they make fun of me, saying, 'Look what a dumb thing he did; let him save himself.'" But sharing the pain of the loss with those close to us gives them the opportunity to admit their own experience with losses not unlike ours.

Henri Nouwen, contemporary theologian, speaks of our being the "wounded healer."[3] Unless we have experienced pain, wounds, even death—either physical death of a loved one or the death of an idea precious to us—we cannot empathize with others. The fact is that everyone is scarred from encounters with life, and the very knowledge of what it's like to be in pain gives us the opportunity to be healers. Reaching out to people who are in Darkness is one very important aspect of healing, our own and theirs.

Though wounded and in pain of soul and body as he was, Jesus nevertheless reached out to those near the cross, trying to make their lives easier, to heal their injured souls . . . the wounded healer. One of his last concerns was his aging, probably widowed, mother. "Mother, behold your son!" "Son, behold your mother!"

"By his stripes we are healed" tells us that the agony of our own "stripes" can make it possible for us to understand the grief of someone else and assist in their healing. The lesson from the cross is that through Jesus' pain, Mary and John met their own pain.

Implicit in the act of "sharing your pain" is the fact that you have to make the first move; you must have faith enough to risk. If you wait for the people around you, even some who are very close, to come to you, it may not happen. Call them, make an appointment, go talk with them, write them a letter. Tell them you are in pain and why. If they reply with an offer to help, let them know what kind of help you need: a listening ear, going out for a cup of coffee or an ice cream now and then, or whatever.

Particularly if they have not gone through something like you are going through, people are likely to be reluctant to offer help for fear it will be the wrong thing, or that they will appear to be prying. People seem to have a singular propensity for avoiding another's pain, not because they do not care, but because they do not know how to handle the situation.

People who have gone through life accidents say they are surprised at the friends or associates who do not appear to offer concern or help, sometimes the ones they were sure would be the first. It is best not to draw any negative meaning from those absences, because the chances are that those people find emotional scenes difficult to handle, and they anticipate such a difficult situation, especially in times of death or divorce. Even if a brother or sister, or close friend—someone usually very close to you—does not show the concern that you need and expect, let it pass.

If you try to determine someone's response beforehand, you may well be disappointed. There may be other things going on in that person's life that prevent him or her from being able to handle your problem, too. Just because you need someone to show caring, it doesn't mean he or she is ready to do that. Trying to manipulate people into a position where they *must* respond to you will not result in the help you really need.

Whether you go to people, or they come to you, it is up to you to let them know what is going on inside your world. Don't make them guess. Since it is a rare person who does not share some secrets, the information that makes the rounds of the community might as well be accurate. Choose carefully your confidants and let them know what is happening.

There is another Confidant in whom you will want to confide your pain. That is God. How do you go about that, especially if you have never been "religious" or felt the need to speak with a spiritual "Being."

For the most part, the problems in our lives are "little"

ones—nuisances, costly in terms of money and time, but not soul-threatening. But many of you reading this book are looking for ways to cope with major upsets. There's nothing small about the loss of a job, your health, your financial security, or your children!

We have talked here about sharing that loss, coming right out and admitting it to those close to you. But how do you do that with God?

One of the best ways is to learn from people who have been through it, and one of the easiest to observe is Job, in the Old Testament.

Now, Job was a good person, not unlike any of us. He was not a "bad" man, and he knew it. Yet awful experiences came his way. His children were killed, his animals destroyed, his servants murdered.

Satan, whose idea this was to test Job, said to God, "Sure, he'll be faithful until it's his own body that is in pain." God told Satan that he could do anything to Job except take his life.

What a miserable time Job had. "He suffered from loathsome sores from the sole of his foot to the crown of his head." Think of the pain caused by one sore on your tongue or a single boil on your hand, and try to imagine Job's condition. He was smelly, filthy, outcast!

Get out the Book of Job and read what incredibly terrible things happened to this man who was no better or worse than you or I.

And don't miss reading what Job did about it. He *raged* at God! No simple prayer and meditation routine for Job! He let God know that all his life he had done the things he was supposed to do. Oh, he wasn't perfect, but he was a God-fearing man.

Job dared to ask, "Why, God? Why?" He went over the whole sad story again and again, thinking about it, talking about it, raging about it! He came close to the God within him and shook his fist in God's face. "Why?" he shouted. "Why should I be punished when I haven't done anything bad enough to lose my children, my farm, my money?"

His friends told him that it was not right to ask to stand close to God, because humans just don't do that, and after all, Job must have deserved to be punished: If he didn't deserve it, it wouldn't have happened to him.

But Job went straight to the one in charge, and the first verse of Chapter 3 says, "Job cursed his day." Make no mistake, Job was raging at God, yes, even cursing Him!

Job wanted to die. Have you ever told yourself in the dead of night that it would just be easier to not wake up tomorrow morning?

Perhaps you object to the use of "rage" or "curse" when talking with God, but this is not a simple everyday problem; this is suicide, the ultimate curse at God!

Job cried that he had no power; that the cards were stacked against him; that there was no hope. How many times have you said that what has happened to you is beyond your control, that "fate" is not on your side, or, "If it weren't for bad luck, I wouldn't be having any luck at all"?

In Chapter Seven, Job really lets go at God. He says that God even gives him terrifying dreams at night. How many times have you wakened, shaking with terror from messages in your dream, and tried to figure out the meaning of your nightmares?

What did Job do about these feelings? In Chapter Seven he says, "I will not restrain my mouth; I will speak in the anguish of my spirit; I will complain in the bitterness of my soul."

And he did!

His pain, his anguish, and his raging went on and on.

Coming out of the Old Testament, you might expect that God struck Job with lightning for daring to defy Him. Instead, God said, "Job, get ready. I'm going to ask you the tough ones. I'll ask the questions and you give the answers.

"Where were you when the earth was made?

"Did you create this universe?

"Who's in control here?"

And, of course, Job was terrified. He said, "I shouldn't have talked to you like that, God. I'm going to put my hand over my mouth and shut up."

But that wasn't what God meant, for only a God who terrifies can save! And God said, "Job, you had the courage to rage at God. Now, let's talk."

And talk they did. When they were through, Job said, "I understand things I didn't understand before. All my life I had heard about you, God. Now I have seen you with my own eyes. Now I really understand that you are in charge."

And God told Job that because he cared enough about the God within him, daring to come close and question his own soul, he was going to have blessings he hadn't known existed.

And it happened! There appeared not just caring friends, brothers and sisters, children, and grandchildren, not just pleasing relationships, as important as they were, but material things—cattle, land, and money beyond his wildest dreams. His health returned, and his energy was renewed.

We are not different from Job.

When the situation is "soul threatening," when to fail the test would mean a loss of your soul and your integrity, then you quit finding stop-gap measures and excuses. Though terrified, you ask the ultimate questions that you would never dare utter, or even have reason to consider, at any other time:

> What does it mean to believe in God when this happens to me?
>
> What do *I* need to do to make this come out right? What does "right" look like?
>
> If I am going to come out of this with my integrity intact, God, what will I do about this decision that is facing me today?
>
> What difference does it make if I live or die, God?

Ask the questions and listen to the answers, for it is the God within you, the Other, who cares the most about what happens to you and is most willing to work closely with you, even while you are crying—or raging.

The unexpected outcome of talking it over with friends or with God is that your body finds release from its burden. The manifestations of our fears—depression, tiredness, headaches, or heartburn—depart, leaving renewed health and vigor. Those weights on your heart and feet are gone, replaced by a spirit willing to try again.

At least twice in the past year I have been so distraught that to rage at God was a relief, for I had nothing to lose, and I discovered that I had everything to gain. The incredible lesson I learned was that the *situation* didn't change; *I did!*

I learned to quit expecting people to come to my rescue; to accept responsibility, not guilt, for what had happened to me.

There is a difference between *responsibility* and *guilt*. Guilt is destructive and drains energy dramatically, leaving you weak and powerless. Accepting responsibility gives a sense of power, the knowledge that you, not fate, are in charge of what happens.

There are several stories in the New Testament that illustrate this graphically. Judas was not an evil man; he thought he was doing the right thing, but when he realized what he had done, his guilt was overwhelming. He did not have what it took to ask pardon for what he considered an unforgivable sin.

> *Still, as of old,*
> *Man by himself is priced.*
> *For thirty pieces Judas sold*
> *Himself, not Christ.*

Peter's denial of Christ was no less ignominious, but instead of giving up, Peter admitted his wrongdoing and returned to become one of the founding fathers of the church.

Through our own failure to see and do what is right, we can come to be the wounded healer, to have compassion for those who fail.

> *Once upon a time I hated him.*
> *But since then I have seen*
> *Men take the price of treachery*
> *And swear their hands were clean.*
>
> *I have seen faith betrayed; have stood*
> *Where peace was bought and sold,*

9

Where truth was bartered for bright coins
   Of silver and of gold;

Judas sinned once, and died self-slain,
   But I—and men like me—
Live on, though every day we set
   Love's feet toward Calvary,

Wax fat, though now and then we flee
   The grief-crowned face of Right—
And sometimes I pray for Judas now
   As any brother might.[4]

The woman whom Jesus met at the well was an outcast in every sense of the term, cast out by society and by her own rejection of herself. When she received the water of life from Jesus, she immediately returned to her village to share it with others. Because Jesus had accepted her as a person of worth, her own image of herself changed. Jesus' willingness to share the living water with her provided the first step toward her transformation from a fear-filled, self-hating woman into a woman freed from her inhibitions, able to initiate a new relationship with the *men* of the village because of her incredible news of salvation. The whole village went to talk to Jesus, to hear for themselves, and said to the woman, "It is no longer just because of your words that we believe, for we have heard for ourselves, and we know that this is indeed the Savior of the world." In the excitement of her new-found freedom to relate to men in a new way, the woman brought the whole community to wholeness.

When I stopped blaming God and bad luck, I was able to reach out to other people and to continue my dialogue with God.

Each time, He said to me, "I'm sorry. I can't change the situation you are in. You created it; you were there every minute of the time; you have to accept the responsibility for it. But because you cared enough to come close enough to rage at God, I want you to know I love you, and because I love you, I am going to give you blessings you never knew existed."

And it happened! The blessings rolled down like ocean waves!

The first time, I was wrapped in a blanket of caring through perhaps the most difficult week of my life by people who would not have reached out to me if I had not raged at God and learned that I had to ask for the cup of cold water and not wait for people to offer it.

The second time, I was actually hoarse from screaming, raging at God for what I thought He had allowed to happen to me. In a white light of insight I learned that there were resources available to me that I had never dreamed of before, and that never again could they be taken away from me.

A writer who knew the truth of this wrote in Isaiah 41, "Everyone helps his neighbor and says to his brother (sister), 'Take courage.'" In that chapter, God says again,

Fear not, for I am with you,
Be not dismayed, for I am your God;
I will strengthen you, I will help you,
I will uphold you with my victorious hand.

If you are suffering from a loss, hiding it will only rob you further of needed strength to cope with the problem. Reaching out is *your* responsibility. Giving the gift of your pain to those close to you and to God will surely result in your receiving a gift in return, the gift of caring love and a spirit freed to soar again.

chapter two

Finding the Path
Inside Yourself

Sometimes we go for years giving little thought to what really
goes on inside ourselves. Then suddenly we are thrown into a
tailspin and must start searching for resources to get us through
the crisis safely. It is a time to crash on the rocky crags of trouble
or discover our own wings and soar above it all.

The Psalmist knew the feeling.

> My heart is in anguish within me,
> the terrors of death have fallen upon me.
> Fear and trembling come upon me,
> and horror overwhelms me.
> And I say, O that I had wings like a dove!
> I would fly away and be at rest.
>
> PSALM 55:4

Not being an introspective person, I never spent long hours
pondering my future or my past, but I did have clearly defined
goals for my life. When suddenly faced with the possible loss of

my thirty-three-year-old marriage, I was shaken to the foundation of my being.

Soon after my husband and I agreed to go for counseling, I came across an idea that altered the course of events for me. Henri Nouwen wrote an article about going to "the desert."[5] He said we must go first to the desert of our lives to encounter Jesus Christ, and then return to the everyday world, fortified with the strength we need. At first I was repelled, even angered, by the idea. I knew that Jesus went to the wilderness to be alone, but that wasn't in twentieth-century America. I didn't have time to go off by myself for days, or even hours!

And even worse was the thought of spending that much time alone. How frightening! I imagined Matthew 19:21 speaking to me: "Go and sell what you own and give the money to the poor . . . then come and follow me." I thought that must surely be what Jesus meant—to leave whatever I was doing and make drastic changes in my life. That's what would be required if I were to go out alone to be with Christ, as Nouwen said we should.

One day, as I was trying to deal with a difficult problem, I wondered how I was going to handle it and meet my other responsibilities at the same time. Exhausted, I felt as if I had worked hard all day, although it was still only morning. I had to drive into town, a trip of about seven minutes. Just as I arrived at my destination, an important insight flooded my brain—the answer to my problem. Suddenly I wasn't tired any more!

As I was rejoicing, I realized that for those seven minutes I had been completely absorbed in thinking about my problem. I had been in my desert, and Christ had been there, too! The verse from Isaiah came to me:

> They that wait upon the Lord shall renew their strength;
> they shall mount up with wings as eagles;
> they shall run and not be weary,
> and they shall walk and not faint.

Out of those few minutes had come strength for the problem facing me at that moment. Isaiah was right! Then I knew that I had been in my desert often and could go there at any time, for a few minutes or for hours.

For some people, going to "the desert" might be prayer; for others, singing, or meditation, as suggested by Jesus in Mark 6: "Come away by yourselves to a lonely place and rest a while." It matters little what it is called, as long as special time and attention are given to looking deep within yourself to discover who you are in relation to God, to what your goals are, and to exploring what could happen at this moment in your life.

Coming out on the other side of a life accident with your soul and psyche still intact requires some careful guidance through the rapids. It is probably best to find the place where you can most easily move into your inner self. It could be in bed after you wake in the morning; in front of the fireplace, with the fire crackling; in your favorite chair, with quiet music; out on a hillside or a hilltop; or while walking your dog.

This sort of contemplation must be done alone, away from other people. A special time is preferable. Get in the habit of reserving that time each day, but be open to entering your desert whenever and wherever you happen to be.

And what do you do in that time in your desert? What does "waiting upon the Lord" look like?

There is a part of us that functions on a different level than the usual conscious mind, often making decisions without our deliberately thinking about it. That part of us knows us better than our conscious mind does and is able to take our total being into consideration.

A woman once told me about that part of herself. In hushed tones, she described the moment when she was in the final throes of taking her own life. The life accident was too much for her. As she stood ready to finish the deed, something, or someone, called her back from the brink. And that someone was part of herself.

What an assurance—that when "you" have given up, a part of "you" that is separate and strong calls you back to safe ground! It is none other than God!

> "Because thou hast made the Lord, which is my refuge,
>   even the most High, thy habitation;
> There shall no evil befall thee.
> For he shall give his angels charge over thee
>   to keep thee in all thy ways.
> They shall bear thee up in their hands,
>   lest thou dash thy foot against a stone.
> I will be with her in trouble;
>   I will deliver her."

PSALM 91

This evokes the concept of "the Word," referred to in the first chapter of the Gospel of John: "But to all who received him, who believed in his name, he gave power to become children of God. And the Word became flesh and dwelt among us, full of grace and truth."

That Being, that Word, that Entity, has contact with the ultimate part of ourselves and with the eternal part of the universe.

Some prefer to be more personal, and so call that "other" part of themselves by another name, even a very personal name such as Margaret or Philip.

Learn to know intimately the other "self" that is within you. Talk with her/him about who you are, about your problem, about your world. This will require intense concentration at first, and is best done when you are free of other intrusions. Don't be surprised when you sense that that "person" is taking an active part in your life.

When my husband and I began to discuss our marriage, I was sure it would be only a short time until everything was fixed up. After all, we would be going to a counselor at last, wouldn't we? Admitting that we needed help was a sure way to cure everything.

But time passed, and when he would not consent to couple counseling, the situation deteriorated rapidly. I found myself spending hours in my desert, not at one time, but a few minutes here, a few minutes there. The second I started the motor of my car to go somewhere, I was deep inside myself.

Over and over, new insights came during those times of deep thought. I found that if I was dragging through my day listlessly, time in my "desert" would send me back, energized, when I needed it the most.

About that time I stumbled onto an idea which helped me learn at a much faster pace; I began to talk aloud.

At first, it was accidental; I did it because I was in pain and needed to hear myself speak; it gave me confidence and seemed to ease the pain. Then, for a while, there were major confrontations with my husband, and I had to be prepared. I would go over possible conversations, gaining new insights and understanding.

It was so effective that I still use the method. Speaking aloud allows me to hear what my ideas sound like, which is often quite different than thinking about them in silence. My friends have learned not to be surprised to find me alone and talking aloud.

More than just speaking, allow yourself to express whatever emotion is waiting to get out. As long as the thoughts are imprisoned in silence, there cannot be full expression. To put feelings into words is to energize them, to turn potential energy into kinetic power.

If it is fear, cry out; if pain, wail; if anger, shout, remembering that God is listening, as he did to the Psalmist who said over and over, "Hear my voice, O God." In the Psalm 77, he is specific: "I cry aloud to God, aloud to God, that he may hear me."

Once, while trying to resolve a difficult problem, I drove out to the country, with the top down on my little '67 Datsun Roadster convertible, shouting into the wind, practicing difficult words and phrases I had never used before but which were absolutely essential to a resolution of the situation. The wind rushing by muted the impact of the message until I could become used to it, for, of course, it was not the words that I had to change, but my concept of the problem. If I could change the words, I could find an alternative model.

The other place to meet yourself in creative encounter is in your dreams.

Craig, a young friend of mine, listened as I talked about the "Other," a skeptical look on his face. But he was going through a difficult time, and was willing to seek help anywhere. One morning soon after he came in great excitement to tell me about his encounter of the night before.

In his pre-sleep period, Craig had tried to contact the Being who was his Other and had searched for the right name by which to call him. No name came to him, and he fell asleep. In his dream he saw a man who told him he was the Other. Craig asked him his name, but the Being said his name wasn't important, that he had come to answer questions. Craig asked the questions that had been bothering him having to do with confrontations to take place the following day. As each question was asked, the Being answered them clearly and concisely.

In the morning Craig remembered each question and each answer, and they were all he needed for the day.

Will you ever forget the feelings you had when your Sunday School teacher told you about Joseph's dreams? How exciting to receive messages in dreams, I thought.

"And Joseph dreamed yet another dream, and said, 'Behold, I have dreamed a dream more.'"

No small message this! His father immediately understood the implications of the dream, as did his brothers, who became extremely angry with him. Because they believed the dreams, they sold Joseph into slavery, a deed which changed the course of the history of Israel.

Although they are a different dimension and not as simple to use as your waking thoughts, dreams are a vital, exciting, helpful part of you that should not be ignored. The dreams that you do not remember are ones you don't need to remember. They can be called "housekeeping" dreams, doing the chores of your mind while you are asleep. The ones you remember are the "unfinished business" of your life.

Have you ever wakened feeling as if you had worked all

night, and remembered dreams that you "worked" through? On the other hand, have you wakened refreshed and renewed, with a reservoir of energy after dreams that seemed to solve some problems? Dreams can be a source of physical rejuvenation.

Are you one of the people who says, "But I never remember any of my dreams"? Each night when you lie down, tell yourself you are going to remember your dreams. Put a paper and pencil beside your bed. If you waken in the night in the middle of a dream or right after one, take up your paper and pencil—don't turn on the light—and write down enough of the dream so that it will stimulate your memory in the morning. Use a large pad so you can write large enough in the darkness not to run into other lines. It will be scribbly, but readable.

The next morning, don't just go over it in your mind; write down all you can remember. You need to do this soon, before you forget, jotting down notes between brushing your teeth and combing your hair. Reserving a special notebook for Dreams will let your inner mind know you are serious about remembering dreams.

But, you say, it is impossible for you to interpret dreams. Difficult, yes, but not impossible. Remember, it is *your* dream; *you* know the meaning. You may need some simple rules of thumb to help you.

1. Dreams have symbols, such as automobiles, rivers, barns, houses, etc.
2. Symbols are based on reality.
3. Each person has within his/her own interpretation.

The most important part of a dream is the feeling, the emotion, you have as you go through it. In a dream I had, I suddenly came upon a dead body, but I felt no fear or ugly feelings. The dead body represented dead ideas, not the death of a person.

Symbols come from real things in your life. A baby is a new idea. Animals, particularly dogs, are almost always people out of your experience.

Dogs are so commonly "human" substitutes that you can be sure the dog in your dream is your friend, your husband, or even yourself. Cats, too, are such a part of the human scene that they represent human characteristics such as companionship or love. Other animals should be interpreted according to how you personally feel about that animal. Are lions powerful rulers? Are snakes deceitful?

I dreamed that someone was clubbing my cat to death, and indeed, in my life just then my ideas were being attacked violently.

Look for the person in the dream who is You. Even though you may feel that you are standing on the outside looking in, you may also be, at the same time, in the scene as one of the actors. And equally surprising, you may be *more* than one person in the same scene.

Automobiles are usually people. Since our cars are really extensions of ourselves, they represent persons, or qualities, in our personalities.

In another dream I had, my son offered to take me for a ride in his boat, so we were floating down a quiet river. But as I watched, the river became wider and wider and more swift, turning into a flood. I looked down and saw that the boat was filling with water.

I said to my son, "Hey! The boat is sinking!"

He replied, "Yes, I didn't want to alarm you."

The boat dropped from under me. I felt myself going down, so I took a big gulp of air and told myself that I was *not* going to panic, but to go down and touch bottom and push myself back up.

Suddenly I bumped into another body in the water, perhaps a dead body; it wasn't moving. I thought to myself, "I can't save him; I can save only myself." I heard other people saying, "Pull him out! He is still alive; maybe we can save him."

I went down to the bottom, pushed myself up, and as I came out of the water, grabbed onto a tree that was sticking out. I was safe!

The dream accurately described my life. The moving stream of my life became a dangerous flood that could overwhelm me, but I took control of the situation and saved myself. The other body in the water was my husband; there was nothing I could do to save him.

If deep within yourself you believe that you are in control, and if in your dreams you save yourself, then in your waking experiences you will also be able to "save" yourself. It is God's way of helping you cope with your world.

If in your dreams you are beaten, overwhelmed, shot, killed, or chased off, that tells you that you are afraid life is going to defeat you. Such dreams can rob you of needed drive. Before you go to sleep each night, give yourself a pep talk, like this:

"When I meet the guy with the gun, or when the fearful creature comes to frighten me, I am going to stand my ground. Instead of running away, I am going to turn and face my attacker."

If you keep telling yourself that, you will do exactly that in your dream. When that happens, you can begin to do the same thing in real life with whatever is threatening you.

Incredibly, as I was writing this chapter at eight o'clock in the morning, my son came from his bedroom, saying, "I just had the most vivid dream." I didn't have to tell him to go on, because he was still in the dream.

My friend and I parked my TR8 convertible in a parking lot. After doing some business in a store, we returned, intending to drive away. Suddenly my friend said, "Stop, don't move!"

String had been tied to the door, across the middle of the car, out the other door and into the shrubs. We followed the lines and discovered they were hooked to explosive devices. To open the car doors would be sure death.

We wanted to get out of there, so we jumped into the car over the top and cut the lines.

Just as I was about to start the car, I became aware of someone behind me, outside the car. I turned. A man was standing there with a black hood on, holding a gun. He shot me four times in the back of the head. Bang! Bang! Bang! Bang! I felt the bullets strike my head.

All of a sudden I stood up in the middle of the car and yelled, "Wait a minute! Where in hell did you come from? This isn't fair! You weren't part of this dream! If you are going to have a gun, I get one too! Somebody give me a gun!"

Now he spoke in the present tense

I'm not really wounded; the bullets didn't kill me. The man in the hood is running off, and strangely, I don't want to chase him.

I'm driving my Triumph and I feel joyous.

For some years this son has been telling me of dreams in which he is killed and watches his funeral procession go by. In the past few months, he has come to believe in his own worth, and his dreams bear that out. He is now ready to challenge the negative parts of himself that would keep him from driving down the road of life in joy and freedom. It has made a big difference in his ability to cope with his world. His feelings of inadequacy detracted from his energy. Now in his dreams he no longer runs away, but stands his ground, and mornings find him ready, instead of holding back, fearful of what the day will bring.

It is believed that all humans, regardless of their culture, have the same basic human concepts that form the foundation of our understanding and are reflected in our dreams. For example, flowing water means change in your life; a building is your life; the rooms in it are specific parts of your life.

Throughout history, dreams have played an important role, especially in the Bible. Pilate, in Matthew's recounting of the crucifixion of Jesus, received word from his wife telling him, "Have nothing to do with that righteous man, for I have suffered much over him today in a dream." That influenced Pilate's decision not to release Jesus, but to merely get rid of the problem, which he tried to do by symbolically washing his hands of the whole affair.

Some dreams can be prophetic.

At five o'clock one morning I wakened suddenly and sat up, terrified. I had just dreamed that at a certain corner in our town I saw a car wreck. Believing the car to be my son's, I went closer, but a bystander assured me it was not. When I saw my son later in the day, I laughingly told him about the dream. A strange look came over his face, and he told me that he had come within a few inches of being killed at that corner early that morning.

In early July I had a dream in which I was walking down a street in Paris, looking for some way through a barrier. Suddenly a way opened. It was a street two blocks long which intersected with a main thoroughfare at the end. As I took a couple steps along the street, I saw a street sign which said *"Aout,"* the French word for August.

Since each person must interpret their own dreams depending on what things mean to them, and I considered Paris my "Shangrila," my "Shining City of Light," my interpretation was that in August I would arrive in my City of Dreams.

On the very last day of August, I did indeed come upon a fantastic new path for myself.

Sitting in my kitchen window is a beautiful hand-blown blue Swedish glass bird that I call my "Bluebird of Happiness," a gift to myself when I was going through a period of Darkness. It became a sign of hope. Recently, I dreamed of a single framed picture of my Bluebird of Happiness broken in two pieces. Awakening immediately, I felt a coldness in my innermost self. Since at that time my life was moving along joyfully and creatively, I wondered at the meaning of the dream. A week later I discovered a lump in one breast!

If your dreams are meaningful to you, you join the long line of people, many of them in the Bible, who through the centuries have been in touch with the Other through their dreams, whose faith has been enriched and strengthened by their dreams. In Deuteronomy and Jeremiah a "dreamer of dreams" is a person of great influence.

What if Joseph had not believed in dreams? "Joseph her husband, being a just man, and not willing to make her a public example, was minded to put her away privately.

"But while he thought on these things, behold, the angel of the Lord appeared to him in a dream saying, 'Joseph, son of

David, fear not to take Mary for your wife; for that which is conceived in her is of the Holy Ghost.

"'And she shall bring forth a son, and you shall call his name Jesus, for he shall save his people from their sins.'"

Abraham, Jacob, Joseph, Mary, Herod, Herod's wife, the Wise Men, and many, many more had dreams that brought a message from God that strengthened their faith.

When Abraham sent Sara, his wife, to King Abimelech, telling the king that she was his sister, God came to Abimelech in a dream and bawled him out for doing a forbidden thing. But Abimelech stood up for himself and talked back to God, who agreed that Abimelech had indeed acted with integrity, since it was Abraham who had caused the problem. The situation was resolved in the dream.

If you are undergoing any one of the many life accidents, don't go it alone. Seek out the Being in your life that is most concerned about you, that cares the most, and knows the most about you—the God within you. Talk with her/him; shout, cry, wail, whatever you need to do, for no one will be more understanding or helpful.

Use your dreams, those self-written plays that portray your innermost self. They are as important in their own way as your waking thoughts, for they can add to or subtract from the store of energy available to you for coping with life.

The journey inside yourself will be the most important and most helpful as you seek to strengthen your faith while moving through your life's plans or life's accidents.

chapter three

Meet Your Own Personal Shetan

"Our fears and anger, as well as our love and faith, come from nowhere but deep inside ourselves. They are our "*shetans*, who can insure a strong faith or drain our reservoirs of energy."

In the cool of the African dry season morning I listened, fascinated, to the man who was speaking. I was in his country as a missionary, to take the "Word" to his people, but in the seven years I was there, I learned as much from him as he did from me. Under the vine where purple grapes hung almost ready for harvest, Mallam Linus sat, his black eyes alive, intense, as he described for me the *shetans*, the demons that live within us, ones that he knew well.

Mallam Linus, the sage of the village, spoke four tribal languages fluently and understood several more. Confined to his compound by tuberculosis, he was nevertheless the center of intellectual activity. Chiefs and servants, young and old, black and white, came to visit with him, to enjoin his wisdom. Ours became a mutual sharing—I from the outside world, and he from the life of the village and the country.

"Our demons are not automatically evil, as I understand they are according to the meaning of *demons* in English," Mallam Linus said. "*Shetans* may be good or evil, depending on what we allow them to be, for they rise up out of ourselves."

"How can that be?" I asked. "What is a *shetan* like?"

"*Shetans* are basic needs or desires with which we are born," he said. "They are neither good nor evil, but we allow them to become good or evil, depending on who we are."

"For example?" I prompted.

He named them one by one.

† Our need for security,
† our desire for physical comfort,
† the need to be loved
† and the need to be close to that which created us;
† the need to become a person separate from every other person in the world,
† and then, we each want to leave behind something that is eternal.

"How are those things *shetans*?" I asked.

"Each one is a basic drive that can drain our energy and destroy our faith in our ability to cope with life, or can give us faith in ourselves, reinvigorating us to face the day's problems.

"In Deuteronomy, chapter thirty," Mallam Linus said, as he picked up the well-used Bible bound in hand-finished leather that lay on the table between us, "the Bible talks of where truth comes from, the truth being God's commandments. The writer says,

"'This commandment which I command you this day, it is not hidden from you, neither is it far off.

"'It is not in heaven . . . neither is it beyond the sea. But the word is very close to you, in your mouth and in your heart that you may do it.'

"I believe," Mallam Linus went on, "this is what the writer

was talking about in the sixteenth chapter of the Gospel of John: 'When the Spirit of truth comes, he will guide you into all the truth.'

"The truth is found within us, and we are responsible for it. Let's take one manifestation of the Spirit, the *shetan* that is the need to separate ourselves from every other person in the world, to be an individual, to be a person of worth. That seems simple enough, but the struggle comes at the point at which we first begin to separate ourselves from the person to whom we were most closely tied, probably our mother, maybe our father. No one has to tell us that to take charge of our own lives we have to separate ourselves from everyone else in the world, beginning with our mother. Somehow we sense that, and even at a very early age, there are battles over who is in charge. Am I in charge of my life, or is my mother?

"Then a few years later Mother accepts the idea that we need to be responsible for ourselves and starts pushing us out of the nest; we establish a relationship with a member of the opposite sex, or with other persons, and the struggle goes on.

"The *shetan* becomes an evil component of our lives when we choose to remain tied to our mother or father, unwilling, and later unable, to stand on our own. The *shetan* is a positive factor when it leads us out into the world to discover our special niche, or to establish homes in which our own children are encouraged to discover their own identities within a circle of love."

The problems in African families were in many ways no different from those in other families of the world, so I continued to ask this very wise friend to share some of his understanding.

"Is it possible for a person to change once the nature of the *shetan* is determined? For instance, can a person whose *shetan* is causing him to remain dependent on his parents change?"

"How old is the person?"

"In his twenties."

Mallam Linus shook his head slowly. "That is one of the most difficult *shetans* to change once the pattern is established. The child who does not very early develop his own faith in God, his own sense of worth, separate from his parents or from his brothers and sisters, seems to have great difficulty doing it later in life." He nodded knowingly. "Trying to convince a child that she is important, that she is loved, by giving compliments or special favors only reinforces the child's belief that she is inferior, because you are treating her differently than you are the other children. She says to herself, 'They don't mean it; they're just telling me that. *I* know I'm not good enough; I don't deserve it.'"

"In other words," I said, "she doesn't know that God loves her."

"Exactly!" Mallam Linus said. "And in those rare moments when people discover and accept the fact that God does indeed love them, that doubting *shetan* is transformed into a trusting *shetan*. It is the moment of transformation from frightened people to people empowered with the energy that comes from knowing they can do it, without depending on someone else, because God is very much present."

"Tell me about the need for physical comfort," I said. "Isn't that a normal facet of life; is it ever evil?"

"When the need for physical comfort becomes a desire to have more than anyone else in the village, it turns into greed."

"I understand," I said, "It is positive when necessity becomes the mother of invention and someone finds a new way to make life easier."

"You're catching on!" Mallam Linus said, his black eyes glowing. "Another *shetan*, the desire to leave behind something that is eternal, is of special concern for the African people. Sometimes I think Americans would rather have it here and now."

"What does that evil *shetan* look like?" I asked.

"Let's talk about the good *shetan* first, the *shetan* that turns us into idealists, that makes us willing to use our zeal on things that will live after us, on helping others live. That is a driving force, a power, that urges us on. But carry that a little further to wanting our name to live forever, and it becomes an energy-draining *shetan*."

"It becomes a self-building drive instead of an other-building drive."

"Right," he said.

"Let's talk about the other *shetan,* the need to relate to a higher force," I said. "I can see that knowing we did not create ourselves would lead us to want to come close to that which did create us, something like a parent."

"But at the same time," Mallam Linus said, "we often get the feeling that *we* are in charge, and we claim as our own all the power of the Creator. As a result, we actually separate ourselves from that power, and instead of being strong, we are weak."

Always our discussions centered around the Bible, and I said, "There is a lot of talk about devils in the New Testament. In Matthew, the Pharisees accuse Jesus of being a devil, but Jesus went calmly on his way. Were those devils *shetans?*"

"There are various meanings of the word devil in the Bible," Mallam Linus said, "In James, the fourth chapter, the writer understands how *shetans* work, for he says, 'Resist the devil, and he will flee from you.' If we understand that *shetans* rise from within us, then we will know that standing our ground, refusing to let them have their way, will eventually cause that *shetan* to be transformed, to be replaced by the positive part of ourselves.

"But it isn't easy." He paused, as if deciding whether to go on, then spoke slowly. "Each one of us has our very own *shetans* that belong to no one else. We cultivate them, direct them, use them. As the result of needing to separate myself from everyone else, to become a person in my own right, I acquired some skills. One of them was the ability to listen to people, sense what was going on in their struggles with their *shetans,* and help them discover insight into what to do.

"But my struggle has been to keep that *shetan* from becoming arrogant and overbearing, telling people what is wrong with them instead of leading them to acquire that insight. It is a good feeling to have the answers, and people are grateful, for many are looking for answers. But I do them no favor if they become dependent on me. There have been times when my self-esteem has declined, and I have needed to have people proclaim how great I was for telling them what to do with their problems. That struggle goes on inside of me."

I watched him continue as teacher and sage, as well as learner, over a period of many years as we exchanged insights. Hearing the Bible discussed from the perspective of a black man in a small village in the African bush opened my eyes to meaningful interpretations of the scriptures.

His eagerness for new ideas, new concepts, never flagged, nor did his willingness to share his own. I will always believe that he lived years longer than he would have, because of an ever-growing faith that renewed his body as well as his spirit.

Now, much later, the memory of those days spent with Mallam Linus recalls the warm memory of a friend, as his concept of *shetans* continues to explain what I see going on around me.

Carrie, a woman married for twelve years, mother of three children, was devastated when she discovered that her husband had found another woman. "But I gave him everything," she cried.

I remembered Mallam Linus' *shetans*.

Carrie's good *shetans*, her need to be loved and her need for security, had led her to accept her father's loving care. Transferring from her father to her husband, little changed except the man involved, and she remained in many ways a child, expecting to be loved and looked after. In return for that, she was willing to present everything she had as a gift to her father, and then her husband. The more she gave away, the more the need to become unique, separate from everyone else in the world, became subordinated. Altering the pattern was even more difficult, since our society rewards women who do what Carrie was doing.

At the same time, her husband, Ralph, began to feel stifled, in bondage to Carrie. He was not unwilling to be the financial support of the family, but he did not need to be Carrie's only emotional brace, for it caused conflict with his own *shetan* that called for individual freedom within the relationship. It was not surprising that he sought another woman who put less pressure on him to provide emotional support, but perhaps his own *shetan* was not strong enough to allow him to talk to his wife. He found it easier to leave the situation than to confront it creatively.

But wasn't that relationship the one he contracted for when he and Carrie were married? Was it fair to change the rules? Marriage should be a garden where the flowers of our spirits can grow and develop, but a garden requires a lot of hard work. When Carrie and Ralph finally began to talk about what was really going on inside themselves, they were amazed to discover how close together were their good and evil *shetans*. Carrie's all-giving love for her father and husband had to be altered to give her more responsibility for herself. Self-care became as important as self-giving. They discovered that each was ready to allow some changes and still remain in the marriage.

Carrie's changes came when she discovered a belief in herself, that is, a belief that God loved her, and from that came a strength she had never known she had.

When Jesus spoke with the woman at the well, it may well have been the first time in her life that a man spoke to her with belief in her potential. Her five husbands had used her need for security to keep her in bondage to them, and she had accepted that role, believing that was who she was. She gave away her power to one man after the other.

Then appeared a man who did not want to take from her, but to give to her, to encourage her to take hold of her own power. That power could be found in living water instead of the water she had been drinking that never satisfied her, compelling her to look for satisfaction in another relationship with yet another man.

Jesus understood her need for security, but also knew she needed a different kind of security, from a right relationship with God.

No wonder she was excited! Jesus helped her turn negative *shetans* into positive ones until she had enough faith to influence a whole community. In spite of a long history of failure, in the eyes of the community as well as in her own, she opened herself to a new way of thinking, and the moment of transformation occurred.

Perhaps one of the best ways to explain the *shetans* within us is to look at a common situation that could happen to any of us.

You go to a dinner for the office staff, one you have been looking forward to, with steak with all the trimmings, provided by the firm. Halfway through the appetizers a person standing near you says something you believe was intended to put you down. Suddenly your stomach knots up, and as soon as possible, you move. But the knot doesn't go away; the evening is ruined. In the middle of the night you waken, feeling ill, you may blame it on "rich" food or the smoked herring.

The next morning at breakfast you are still seething, your body tense, your hands even shaking a little.

There you sit, extremely angry, without another person in the room! Where is your anger coming from? From the person who made the remark? Hardly, he isn't anywhere near. It is coming straight up out of yourself; it is your *shetan*. Your worth as a person has been challenged; your faith is faltering, and your response is to allow yourself to become threatened and angry. As your power is drained away, you blame someone else.

Let us alter the picture. The night before, you had gone to the party in a good mood, ready to enjoy good food and good company. When the person made the remark, you said to yourself, "Doug must be in a bad mood tonight; I'm not going to let his bad mood ruin my good mood." That would have been the end of that.

The next morning at breakfast you would have been calmly enjoying your second cup of coffee, your faith strong, your belief in your own worth still intact, your energy available for the day's task instead of flailing at windmills.

Jesus did exactly that for the woman at the well. Her husbands put her down, but through Jesus the woman could realize and release her hidden strength and faith.

Dreams are a good place to discover our *shetans*, for the

subconscious is the place they are formed. In my son's dream in which the figure in a black hood shot him, the *shetan* of the need for personal security was being formed. He overcame the fear that his *shetan* would render him unable to continue at the wheel of his own car driving down his road.

We do have control over the *shetans* within us, but we must not underestimate their power to drain vital energy. Maintaining our strong faith in God, we can program those *shetans* to help us become whoever we want to be!

chapter four

The Highest Goal

In each of my moments of Darkness, the words of God to the people of Israel have brought strength and encouragement. "Today I present to you life and death. Therefore, choose life!"

How does one go through a soul-threatening experience and come out of it whole, with faith still intact and strength enough to pick up the pieces and go on?

We have talked about several important ideas that can help.

Watching Carol, a close friend, go through a life accident helped me discover another concept, one of the most important because it is a guideline to faith that can help us through our individual crises.

Carol lives some distance away, in another town, but we communicate fairly often by telephone. However, she went through this life accident by herself, and then shared it with me later.

Carol was terminated at her job suddenly, without notice, when the recession forced massive cutbacks by the company. Even though some of the people laid off had been with the company for as long as twenty-five years, that was little comfort for Carol. She told the story to me like this:

"I came home in a blue daze and collapsed in the first chair I came to in the front room. Thank goodness, no one was home.

"What were we going to do? We needed my income!

"Jim and I had talked about the possibility of layoffs, so it would not come as a surprise to him, but we would have to break the news to the children. It would mean not doing some of the things we had promised and planned on, such as buying a new cello for Rick . . .

"I would have to start looking immediately for another job. The thought of that sent cold spikes of fear through me. Looking for another job, after being with this company for nine years? And in this time of high unemployment?

"I had been dry-eyed up until then. Maybe it was from the shock. But suddenly I began to cry, and I realized that I was angry, *very* angry. Jim has never been paid what he was worth (Jim works at the small private college where he is registrar), but he stuck with his job because he felt it was important. I was suddenly furious that he had never been paid enough to support the family, which was why I had gone to work in the first place. And we certainly do not have a high-priced life style.

"Then I realized that besides being angry, I was afraid—afraid I wouldn't be able to find another job, but, more than that, that I, Carol, would not be able to measure up. 'Measure up to whom?' I asked myself. To younger women, better qualified women, men, all competing for jobs.

"Losing my job had stripped me of my self-assurance, my self-respect; I felt threatened to the very core of my soul. And I was more than a little angry with God.

"And then I remembered what we had discussed the last time we were together, about going to the 'desert' as Jesus did when he was in need of some answers. So I went to my desert, sitting there in that chair, and after demanding that God listen to me, I began talking out loud. I said, 'Carol, how are you going to come out of this in one piece? You could call Jean and talk about this, but when the chips are down, *you* are the one who has to do it.'

"'Do what?' I said to myself. 'Carol, what is your goal? What is the best that could come out of this situation?'

"I thought about that and finally said, 'I want my children and friends to see me handling this with courage and faith; I want Jim to be proud of me; I want to be proud of myself! In other words, I want to come out of this with my integrity intact.'

"I liked that goal, *to come out of this with my integrity intact*. I think God took time to answer my prayer.

"So I decided that from that moment on I would slow down, take one step backward and set my eyes on that goal. Every time I had to make a decision, I would measure it against that goal, the goal of maintaining my integrity."

When I received Carol's letter, I called her immediately and then sent her the verse from Psalm 26:

> But as for me, I walk in my integrity;
>   redeem me, and be gracious to me.
> And I have trusted in the Lord without wavering.
>   I will walk in faithfulness to thee.

Not long after that I had reason to use Carol's experience in my own life, and I realized that "goal" that we set our sights on was God. We were calling ourselves to the highest understanding that we knew. For me, that was the covenant I had made with God when I became a Christian, which I renewed now.

The Psalmist said, "Let integrity and uprightness preserve me; for I wait on Thee."

What does integrity look like?

It does not mean giving up just because hanging in there might cause an uncomfortable situation for you or for the other person. Doing what you have to do for yourself at that moment in your life, that is integrity. It does not mean settling for less at the moment to avoid "hurting" another person. But can doing something that is going to hurt someone else be integrity?

Let's look closer at such a situation.

Let us say you have gone out of your way to do something for your husband. Something you have done before that was pleasing to him. But this time, for some reason you could not have known, he doesn't like it at all. Do you think that you should have done something different, been more sensitive? Was it really your fault that he was angry? He has chosen to be angry about that.

Turn the situation around. Your friend is very upset with you and does something she knows will make you angry. But that day you had decided you weren't going to let anything bother you. It was a great day, one you wanted to remember as the day you allowed yourself to be supremely happy. So when your friend does her thing, you simply say, "I'm not going to get angry; I'm just going to ignore that."

We choose whether or not events in our life will make us happy or unhappy. Remember, it is not what happens to us that makes the difference, but what we do with what happens to us! We must accept responsibility for our lives. If we constantly blame "luck" or "fate" or another person, we are giving away our power, diminishing our drive, leaving ourselves feeling weak and frustrated.

Accepting responsibility for our anger or happiness means believing in God's promises to be with us. This gives the power to *us*, and that energy is available for us to use.

What we are at this moment is what we programmed into our psyches months and years ago. Sometimes we reach goals we didn't even know we had; they were hidden deep inside ourselves, possibly from early childhood.

The sixth chapter of *Ephesians* describes this in other terms:

Whatever a man sows, that shall he reap.
For he who sows to the flesh shall of the flesh reap
    corruption,
But he that sows to the Spirit shall of the Spirit reap
    life everlasting.

Anything that was learned can be unlearned. But no one says it will be easy to "unlearn" an image that was set soon after we were born.

In the book *Stress, Power and Ministry*, the author says, " . . . you can divide men and women most fundamentally into two classes—those who are fear-determined and those who are love-determined. The ones who are fear-determined are sunless. They have no sun in themselves and go about putting out the sun in other people. They are the people Jesus said needed to be reborn. Whereas the love-determined people have life in them, abundant life, and they turn towards life and fight for life against the forces of death."[6]

We set those goals without consciously realizing that we are fear-determined or love-determined, but set them, we do. It is not difficult to discover which type you are. When someone reaches out to you, do you respond by pulling back or reaching out?

The writer of *I John* understood this when he said, "If we love one another, God is in us," and, "He who dwells in love dwells in God and God in him."

The way to get rid of fear, as given by the writer of I John, is to have love, for "perfect love casts out fear." It is not easy if the pattern has been there for years; changing fear into faith can happen only if you realize the need to do so, set it as your goal, and work toward it.

Women, especially, have a problem in deciding what integrity looks like. Women often back off and give up, rather than go against the wishes of the men in their lives. Programmed from girlhood to be a psychological support to the man who is maintaining them financially, they think if they just go on being the care-giver, their men will see to it that they are looked after.

How many times I have heard divorced women say, "I would rather have my children than fight for money." A laudable thought, but one that is rarely rewarded by society despite its claims to the contrary. Five years after the divorce, woman after woman finds that her children are doing without necessities because she chose not to fight for a realistic share of the financial resources she helped put together in the marriage. That is beginning to change, but very slowly.

Rather than appear grasping and hard in the eyes of their friends or children, these women settle for far less than they need or deserve in job opportunities or monetary recompense. Above all, women do not want to appear unfeminine. They would rather be "liked" than to win, and in the process they give away the power they need to use their gifts most effectively.

The stress that comes from having the financial and nurturing responsibility of children, often without paying adequate attention to their own needs, drains energy. Many women speak of "sleeping poorly," of being tired. At a time when they need the most stamina to handle a job as well as cope with their children's needs, they often feel inadequate. It may even show in their faces.

While writing this chapter, I had occasion to go through several large airports with some hours to wait between flights. Since people are the most interesting pastime of all, and having just read the article on fear-determined and love-determined people, I started studying people's faces, particularly of people traveling alone.

When people are in an airport, they are between worlds. No one knows them, and they know no one; they are themselves, free of pretense. Who they are, deep inside, is reflected on their faces.

A man who has been a grouch all his life, that is, fear-determined, without a sustaining faith, has the lines to prove it, lines that make his mouth turn down. Even if his journey is a happy one, his underlying unhappiness is evident in his face.

The woman who has always been an optimist, believing in a caring God, cannot hide her love-determined self, even if her journey is a sad one.

Our faces reflect our innermost selves, a photograph of our souls projected onto the screen of our faces.

The way people approach or respond to a stewardess or an airline clerk speaks eloquently to whom they are at heart, for there is no one around for whom they must act out a role. Their innate surliness or outgoingness is up front for all to see. It is especially at places such as airports that a cigarette becomes a protective barrier between a person and the other people "out there." Contrast that to a child, whose face is open, trusting, meeting your eyes, his curiosity and wonder opening the path between him and other people. But if he is fear-determined, in a few short years he too will be finding ways to hide; if he is love-determined, he will be enjoying the experience of reaching out and learning to know the God that is within other people.

The story of Herod comes readily to mind. A fear-determined person, Herod ordered the death of thousands of children who threatened his fear-determined kingdom. Because of his sick fear, Herod committed one of the most infamous acts of all time, killing babies in order to get Jesus.

Setting a goal, clearly stating to yourself where you want to be at a specific point down the road, will allow you to measure all steps against that vision. A love-determined goal may just bring the sunshine of God's presence into the lives of many with whom you interact.

The common emotions of fear, anger, and pain are so immediate and so strong, draining energy to cope with them, that the only way to maintain a perspective beyond them is to have a vision that rises above them, solid and visible, rooted in faith. It is with relief that you raise your gaze and see, unmoving and solid, the image of the person you want to be. Then each decision will be easier because you can feel yourself coming, step by step, closer to the goal, the "high calling" you have set.

Let the Apostle Paul be our example.

*I think I have not yet arrived, but setting aside
all that is behind, I press forward to the high calling which is
Christ Jesus our Lord*

PHILIPPIANS 3: 12-14

chapter five

Celebrate the Beginnings and Endings of Our Lives

Inevitably you must come face to face with the final moment of death, the last day of the job, a relationship irrevocably broken, or a move demanding that you walk out of the house where you have lived for years. How can you do that without falling apart, without great anger or overburdening pain or, more important, without losing the faith so vital to wholeness?

A young woman, Pat, taught me a very important lesson about beginnings and endings. This is her story.

My friend, Virginia's leaving was at an unfortunate moment in our relationship. She and I had been through almost everything together; the birth of our children, their growing up years, their difficult teen years, our marital ups and downs. Transferred with her family to another town, she was giving up her own job so her husband could accept a significant promotion.

We had recently had a disagreement. We had had disagreements through the years, but we had always ironed them out, each time becoming closer friends. Given a few weeks, this one could have been worked out too, but there wasn't time; she was leaving the next day.

It was one of those situations in which we were both right and both wrong—and both stubborn.

That day I could accomplish nothing; turning from one task to another, I didn't have the energy to complete even the simple ones. Virginia was my best friend; how could I let her go without this being settled? She was upset at having to leave her job and her home of many years, yet excited for her husband. I told myself this was no time to try to deal with our relationship, but I knew it was an excuse. As the day wore on, I became more and more weary.

When I happened to pass the big map of the United States on the wall of my son's room and noticed how far away Virginia would be, that did it. I had to do something to assuage my pain and feelings of guilt before Virginia left. Letters and telephone calls are poor substitutes.

What could I do in the short time we had? The rift was so deep that we were not going to be able to resolve it quickly. Even if we both said we were sorry, it would still take time to work through the pain and anger. Yet I could not let her go without some kind of farewell. If I could not do something about this most important of relationships, how could I consider myself a Christian? I remembered my pastor had said we should celebrate the beginnings and endings of our lives. An idea came to me and I quickly wrote something down.

Then I drove to Virginia's house.

I guided her into the family room and shut the door. Not at all sure how she would accept what I was doing, I said fearfully, "Virginia, there is something I would like for us to do together."

She said nothing, only nodded, and we sat down, stiffly, on two chairs.

I did not have to read from the paper; I said it from my heart:

"You are leaving, and I am staying . . .

There are misunderstandings that apparently cannot be healed just now . . .

But I cannot live with bitterness, anger and hate,

So let us recognize that

Each of us has done what we had to do because that's who we were just then . . .

And let us forgive each other and ourselves.

Let's remember the beautiful things between us . . .

. . . When you sat with me through John's surgery,

. . . When I helped you make Elisabeth's wedding gown because you couldn't see through your tears,

. . . When we cheated on our diets with hot fudge sundaes.

Let us put the beautiful things of this relationship on the shelf of our hearts,

Safe from the ravages of anger.

And let us part in peace."

When I finished, I stood up and went to her, and we held each other, crying together.

"Goodby," I said, and she repeated, "Goodby."

I have been glad many times over that we had the Celebration, for it allowed both of us to deal with a moment that otherwise would have been awkward and unbearably painful.

But more important, I felt as if I had been faithful to my vow to God. When I got home, I was so relieved, so freed, so revived, that I made a cherry pie for supper. And the poster on my kitchen wall suddenly took on new meaning, the one that says:

"He sets the prisoner free, opens the eyes of the blind, and lifts those who are bowed down."

I wish I could say that later our friendship was renewed as it was before, but within a couple months, Virginia was killed in an automobile accident. What if I had not had the courage to go to her with the Celebration of our faith in each other?

What courage! What a freeing experience! It returned to Virginia the power that had been drained away by anger.

When she told me this story, I thought of the passage in Mark, when Jesus said, "Daughter, your faith has made you well; go in peace and be healed." Not only was her physical world improved, but her relationship with the Eternal was restored also.

Rollo May, writing in *Love and Will*, says, "Accept it, breathe with it, run toward it, not away. Strangely enough, it has lost its power. Anxiety or fear or anger has the upper hand as long as we continue to run."[7]

It is not the actual event that causes the problem; it is the fear or pain that we expect to feel as we go through the event. So to face the fear or pain head-on is to remove from it its power over us.

It is possible to decide that the situation or condition (your spouse's anger; your friend's leaving; accusations) is not going to be allowed to hurt you, for we have the power to choose to what extent we will be hurt. But a rite or celebration can put the situation in terms you can get hold of. It is the unknown that frightens us. Planning ahead to perform a rite at the parting of friends, for whatever reason, will make it less painful, less emotionally draining.

The idea of "celebrating" beginnings and endings, of holding up the elements of our faith at times of emotional peaks, can be adapted to many instances. One of the most important is happy occasions, such as birthdays, graduations, promotions, achievements. Grasp every moment to derive pleasure from little or big events. It helps balance our lives.

In the midst of great affliction, stopping for a celebration of joy can make the pain bearable, or at the very least take our minds from it for a little while.

Let us apply this idea to some of the events and life accidents that you are facing or will face sometime.

Religious rites are not actually for the purpose of following tradition, as most of us believe. They originated out of needs of the human community and have become traditions precisely because they filled a need. We can take a lesson from such traditions and adapt them to our individual or family needs.

When a close friend is leaving, there must be a ceremony of farewell—at the very least, the hug and the kiss. But how often even that is omitted. Have you ever watched young people going off to college or the arrival of Grandmother after a two-month absence? So many times there is no physical touching, only words. Studies have shown the importance of touching, and yet we remain aloof from each other, unwilling to witness to our faith in each other, not tapping the sources of energy that are available in relationships.

Have you seen the posters that show a furry puppy saying, "I don't need much love, just a constant supply" or the saying "I can last a whole week on one hug"? Touching is important.

When boys reach the age of five or six, we begin to withdraw from touching them, as if that would somehow make them less able to go out into the world and do the job men are supposed to do. In removing touching, which to a child is evidence of love and caring, we take away the very element that would make the child more able to cope with his world. We teach him to be separate from the other people around him, to relate in cold, carefully-controlled ways. It is no wonder that so many men fear intimacy and their wives and children feel emotionally under-nourished.

If the situation is a time of great trauma, then it would be wise to share more than a hug. A simple statement of farewell read aloud will cement the friendship, for how will each of you know how the other feels except by putting it into words and actions?

Too often we do not express our emotions, hoping other people will somehow know the depth of our caring, or the extent of our suffering.

In all loss there is guilt, a feeling that we didn't do our best, or acted in unbecoming or even hateful ways. What better way to assuage guilt than to put it into words, if only in the privacy of your own room?

If you have the courage to talk about your less-than-perfect actions, it opens the way for the other person to do the same. Or you may need to be ready to encourage reconciliation if you are the aggrieved person.

Ellen wrote a sharp note to Jane, criticizing her for something Jane had, in fact, not done. Rather than try to explain and add fuel to the fire, Jane merely replied that when there was time, perhaps the two of them could sit down and talk about it.

Months passed, and in the meantime, Ellen learned that Jane had not done what she had accused her of. The relationship was still strained; whenever they were together, the memory of those sharp words hung between them, but Jane kept hoping that something could be done, because in one corner of her soul was a nagging pain that would not go away. One day the two women were cast together in a committee, and Jane realized this might be the time to open the door to reconciliation.

When the opportunity presented itself, Jane made a reference, not to the original event, but to a situation bearing a resemblance. Ellen took the opportunity to say, "Jane, some time ago I wrote a letter criticizing you unfairly. I want you to know that I didn't understand everything about the situation. Now I know better."

Jane accepted the apology; the wall between them lifted and the nagging pain disappeared.

As difficult as that appears, and as tough as it is to do, when it is over, if you were the one to take the initiative, you have a feeling of power, a feeling of being in charge, instead of being the "victim," of allowing outside forces to determine the course of events in your life. Standing back, waiting for the other person to make the first move or to apologize, casts you in the role of the victim, a self-defeating situation.

As a result of such a resolution, the need to separate our feelings into "she" and "I" or "they" and "we" is no longer there. And it helps to bring to an end the loss of vitality caused by continuing anger. Anger forces us to use vast quantities of energy that would be better spent on positive actions.

What a joyous moment it is when you take the step that frees you from the bondage of resentment, when belief in the possibility of loving relationships again returns, for we do take seriously the commandment to "love one another." It is when that commandment is broken that we have the most soul pain. But fulfilling that commandment is so difficult!

In the story of Pat and Virginia, one of the most significant results of the event was forgiveness. Since so much of our anger and pain comes from guilt, dealing with the situation causing the guilt can allow us to forgive ourselves, a prerequisite to a healthy mind and spirit.

The importance of forgiving ourselves is curcial if we are to have the drive necessary for our normal activities. Holding a grudge drains our power.

But what is the mechanism of forgiving?

Forgiveness is one of the least understood but most important aspects of our lives. There are perhaps more sermons on that subject than any other. In the past, they seem to say that forgiving is just something you do, like buying a candy bar or writing a check to pay a bill. Now I wonder if the real message was there but fell on ears not yet ready to understand.

In a moment of need I discovered the mechanism of forgiving. In no event is there a longer list of grievances than in divorce, but fortunately I had a friend who did not let me wallow in self-pity. Our conversation went like this:

"Several years ago when you were still trying to work on the relationship, John wouldn't talk to you and sometimes you became angry and lost your temper. That only made things worse. Why didn't you stop doing that?"

I thought about that a little and replied, "I couldn't. I didn't know what I know now about how to express my pain to John."

"And you couldn't have done any differently?" my friend asked.

"No, I couldn't have. That's who I was at that moment."

And suddenly I knew what forgiveness looks like. I could forgive John for refusing to talk about the relationship because that's who he was. But more important, I could forgive myself. We both were who we were at that moment in our lives. If we could have done differently, we would have.

That bit of crucial insight opened the way for me to prepare a Celebration For the Ending of the Marriage, in which we both participated. It stated that we could forgive each other for being who we were. That allowed us to move on instead of spinning our wheels in anger and resentment, waiting for the other to apologize.

The mechanism of forgiveness is to accept the fact that each of us is who we are at that moment. If we could be different, we would. That allows us to accept, without condoning, the actions of the other person, and also to accept responsibility, without guilt, for our own actions.

Putting the act of forgiveness into words is a freeing experience. If it is impossible for you to express them to the other person involved, at least do it by yourself as an act of healing.

Forgiving restores your faith in a loving God, for if you can forgive the other person and yourself, that opens the door for God's forgiveness. There are few experiences so empowering as that of accepting that God has forgiven you. A whole new world of joy opens up, a gift just for you.

By grace you are saved through faith;
it is the gift of God.

EPHESIANS 2:8

The sudden loss of a job does not sound like the time to "celebrate." But, in fact, calling the family together and daring to look the situation in the face can make it much easier for everyone to accept and deal with it, particularly for small children who normally see only the fear and frustration in their parents' faces and actions. Faith is tested severely at such times; one's children need to see faith being acted out.

Certainly Abraham's faith that led him to what we would consider extreme obedience in being willing to sacrifice his own son because he believed that was what being faithful meant, was an example that Isaac would never forget.

The angel said, "Because you have done this, I will bless you . . . and in thy seed shall all the nations of the earth be blessed; because you obeyed my voice."

This is a suggested Celebration in Time of Loss:

Read Isaiah 40:29-31 which says, "They who wait for the Lord shall renew their strength," and Lamentations 3:22.

The steadfast love of the Lord never ceases,
his mercies never come to an end;
they are new every morning;
great is thy faithfulness.

Then you can say:

The family has been called together

So that each of us may be part of the pain of the loss of Father's (Mother's) job . . .

The loss of money is frightening,

The loss of meaningful labor is frustrating.

But this has happened to us all, not just to Father (Mother.)

Let us talk about how we feel about this event.

Give time for each member to respond.

Each of us will have a responsibility to do our part to make this difficult time easier.

Let us think about what our share of that will be . . .

Give time to meditate.

Let us each describe what will be our part . . .

Give time for each to respond.

We are a family, and we will go through this together, as a family!

In spite of this loss, our love and caring for each other will not diminish.

Pray together for God's continued presence with your family.

When the loss is health, we are dealing with a different problem, and yet, our illness is often tied closely to other things going on in our lives, as we will see in Chapter 10. Illness is a time of faith-testing.

James told the Brethren what to do in time of crisis.

> *Is anyone among you suffering? Let him pray. Is any cheerful? Let him sing praise. Is any among you sick? Let him call for the elders of the church, and let them pray over him, anointing him with oil in the name of the Lord; and the prayer of faith will save the sick man, and the Lord will raise him up; and if he has committed sins, he will be forgiven.*
>
> *Therefore confess your sins to one another, and pray for one another, that you may be healed. The prayer of a righteous man has great power in its effects.*

JAMES 5:13-16

Some churches have an anointing service which is a Celebration for Healing. Anointing is done for three purposes:

1. to activate the healing force
2. to receive a new start after a traumatic negative life experience
3. to prepare for death[8]

By all means, ask for that if your church provides it, but if you do not have access to such a rite, make up your own.

It might look like this:

> We gather together in body and spirit to activate the health force.
>
> Read a favorite scripture such as John 15, James 5 or Psalm 42.
>
> A prayer of Confession and Preparation
>
> A statement of Faith
>
> Anointing with oil

Laying on of hands and prayer for activating the health force. "It is peace that we seek, peace within ourselves, with each other."

"Oh, God, release within me my own healing force that I might be at peace. Then I shall know the wholeness that is available to me. Amen."

A prayer, or the Lord's Prayer, with all present joining hands with the person receiving the anointing.[9]

Now you can begin to see why touching and hugging are so important in human relationships. It gives us a handle to keep our emotions in control while we are going through a beginning or an ending. The person who avoids hellos and goodbys is actually bringing on more pain rather than less. And each time we touch or kiss a lover, a friend, a member of the family, we strengthen the relationship.

Hugging and kissing are actually rites for the purpose of establishing and nourishing human relationships. Each kiss is in itself a Celebration.

A simple but significant rite that can be a faith statement uttered silently to yourself, or used as an affirmation with others in times of joy or sudden crisis, is this:

"Today is the Celebration of the victory of our God,
Thanks be to God!"

In such an affirmation we are saying that in God we can discover a creative response to everything that happens to us— good or bad.

With God, we are winners!

A deliberate stating of our pain, our joy, our fear, will give those involved in separation or loss a feeling of not being swept along by uncontrolled circumstances. Rather, a rite of celebration can give a sense of stability, of power, of direction, of intentionality, and an opportunity to express faith in God.

You may need to be the person of strength and courage who leads the way.

chapter six

Envisioning

Unless you can envision something in your mind, you will never be able to create it.

Unless you believe something can happen, it cannot happen.

Unless you have a clear picture of what you are looking for, you won't recognize it when it appears.

Before Jesus made a move to heal the paralytic at the pool of Bethesda, he first asked, "What do you want?"

Did the man really want to be healed? It would be a complete change of life. He would suddenly have to be responsible for his food and shelter. Whereas before he had been given alms and food, he would now be required to work for a living. Was he ready for that, or would he really prefer to remain a cripple? Jesus was deliberately probing to discover the man's goal for his life.

You are in the midst of a life accident—loss of a job, a friendship, financial security, your marriage, your health. If you sit back and wait to see what will happen, you have only yourself to blame for the results. You may actually choose to remain a cripple.

How many people blame what happens to them on someone else, on fate, on luck, on circumstances beyond their control.

Karen, a woman I know, has been divorced for several years. Still bitter about being rejected and being treated unfairly in the financial settlement, she blames everything that happens to her on someone or some thing. Recently her former husband sent her $1,000. That very week her car fell apart, costing $700 to repair. To some, that would appear to be just bad luck or "circumstances beyond her control." In reality Karen set herself up for that. The largest portion of her energy is spent hating her former husband, checking to see who he is living with now, berating him in front of the children and crying to her friends.

She was treated grossly unfairly in the divorce settlement, but at the time she could not even balance her own checkbook. Reluctantly, she learned some of the rudiments of finance. Over and over she reinforces the image she has of herself as a cripple, a victim of her husband, of life, of circumstances. That includes taking care of her car; she hopes someone will do that for her.

Every time the car wouldn't start, she could prove again that if her husband had not run off with another woman, or if the mechanic had done the job right, or if the court had just given her a fair settlement, her life would not be in the mess it is in. There is enough truth in her complaints to validate her anger. In the meantime her friends drop away, unwilling to scold her when she already has enough problems. Becoming increasingly lonely, she compounds her ills. As long as she needs the feeling of being the victim, she will continue to be a victim, for *we give up only that which we do not want*. The man at the pool decided to give up being a cripple in exchange for a less secure but rewarding new life.

The story of the relationship between Judas and Jesus is tragic because Judas could never believe that love was the most powerful force in the world, and he contrived to bring about

Jesus' Kingdom by manipulating Jesus. Surely, with the power that Jesus spoke of having, he would strike dead the people who came to take him away. When Judas saw love in action, he hanged himself.

Contrast Judas with Peter. When Peter saw that disloyalty to Jesus had caused pain to the person he loved, he wept bitterly. But he had learned what love looks like, and after Pentecost, Peter stood up for Christ, even unto his own death, refusing to let a mistake, even one that big, cripple him for life—or death.

Another woman, Marie, was left with four children and a minimum of support from her attorney husband, who married again and felt little responsibility for his children. This woman is a role model to others going through the trauma of divorce. She has every reason to be angry because each month is a struggle to pay the bills. But Marie has an image of herself that she is striving to bring to reality, that of being self-sufficient, happy and a good mother. She does not make excuses for her former husband, but she does not spend effort berating him either. She is using the lessons she learned about finances to insure that her successful image of herself will come true.

But the underlying factor that has made her image possible is her regular attendance at mass, for as she said, "Without my faith, I wouldn't be able to keep going."

I can do all things through Christ which strengthens me.
PHILIPPIANS 4:13

Whoever you are at this moment in your life is the person you envisioned in your mind over the years. The best way I can describe Wilbur is that about fifty years ago he put himself into a slow-drying plaster cast of fear and self-hate. Now in the middle years of his life, when he should be enjoying the fruits of his labors and visions, he is a frightened man, desperately trying to find happiness. His method is to change the woman in his life and to consolidate his finances. Too late he will discover that his plaster cast has hardened, because his vision of seeking happiness through another person or via money is clearly described in Deuteronomy 8, where the message from God was, "Beware lest you say in your heart, 'My power and the might of my hand have gotten me this wealth.' You shall remember the lord your God, for it is he who gives you power to get wealth; that he may confirm his covenant with you."

The course you are choosing now will determine who you are ten years from now. Why not set your sights on the highest you know? Why not be the person you always wanted to be?

How do you go about it? By envisioning what that person is like. Write it down, in specific detail, not in terms of wishful thinking but in terms of faith that it can happen. Say in present tense, "I am . . ."

1. I am successful as an (accountant, businesswoman, salesman . . .).
2. I earn $____ a year. (Be generous with yourself.)
3. I have a close, loving relationship with ____.
4. As part of my covenant with God, I will give $____ to the church (charity) each week (month). (Be generous with God.)
5. I take care of this body, God's temple, by . . .
6. I weigh ____ pounds.

Be assured that God is as concerned about what you weigh, who your friends are, or what job you have, as you are, so don't hesitate to include everything that is important to you. If you have been discouraged and tired, you will be surprised at the sudden sense of new spirit as you state belief in your future.

Write them all down, fifty of them if you like. These are your *Affirmations.* Each morning before you get out of bed, repeat them over to yourself, and each evening as you are falling asleep, say them again.

Don't list anything that you are not prepared to have happen. I decided I had nothing to lose, so why not try it? So I made my list and faithfully repeated it morning and night, and a few times in between. One of them was "I earn $30,000 a year." Within two weeks I was offered a job that paid $32,000 a year, but I was not expecting it and thought only of the obstacles that I could throw in the way to avoid taking any risks. My husband would be angry if I was gone that much. I might not be able to do the job. Did I really want that job? Too late, I realized that one of my affirmations had come true within two weeks! I hadn't recognized it, in spite of the fact that I had been saying the Affirmations morning and night!

I had changed my goal but had not altered the image that I had of myself. Such a situation puts our stated affirmations into direct conflict with the image we have programmed into ourselves.

After her divorce, Mildred was doing very well in real estate, developing a reputation for being a "smart" saleswoman and an agent who could "get your property sold if anyone can!" Whenever we had lunch together, she spoke of the bright future in real estate that she envisioned for herself. Into her life came a man who seemed to be just what she was looking for, someone to marry her and look after her for the rest of her life. The relationship became very serious. She was ecstatic and made elaborate plans for their future, plans that did not include her continuing as a realtor. She began putting in fewer hours at work, which caused her finances to suffer.

Then her friend failed to appear for one date, and then another, and finally called off the relationship altogether. Devastated emotionally, Mildred was also in deep trouble financially. She had never altered the image of herself as the wife of a man who would look after her, putting her faith in someone else instead of the God within her.

After Frank's wife died, he struggled with housekeeping chores and kept saying, "But I can't cook; I can't keep a house clean." Every time he expressed that, he was making an affirmation, one that prevented him from learning even the basics of looking after his needs. He met a woman and immediately decided she was to be his wife. Neglecting all care of the house, he kept telling himself that he would be married soon, and she would take care of the home. Six months later she gave him a final "No." He had tied all his hopes of something outside himself over which he had no control. What a mess his kitchen was by that time!

In actuality, the envisioning process is going on within our psyches all the time; we are just not in conscious control of it. If you decide to be consciously in charge of your life from now on, it can be a delightful experience to watch your plans and dreams unfold before your eyes.

No longer will you sit around and wonder what is going to happen or lament what is happening. *You* will be making it happen. A man told me that he traveled into many countries and into many jobs and situations, trying to find "the action," until he decided to make his own action.

Remember, you can't see ahead if you are looking backward.

Paul was such a deliberate, future-creating person. His goals clearly in mind, Paul would say, "I must . . .," and, " . . . forgetting those things which are behind, and reaching forth unto those things which are before, I press toward the mark for the prize of the high calling of God in Christ Jesus."

Jesus had clear goals, saying, "I must work the works of him that sent me, while it is day; the night cometh, when no one can work." No amount of drive will be effective if it is available at the wrong time. Set goals and be ready with the necessary skills and strength now, while it is day.

As a result of the inevitable problems and crises in our lives, there are times when we seriously question whether we can retain our sanity, for it appears that our world is falling apart, even that *we* are falling apart.

In the twelfth chapter of Hebrews, the writer says, "Sometimes God shakes the world to discover that which is unshakeable."

Being shaken may be incontrovertible proof that you are alive, that God is still there challenging you to settle for nothing less than your best. Before the moment of crisis comes, look up, reconfirm your faith and set your goals; then affirm them every day until they come true.

chapter seven

We Are Always Five and Fifty-five

We strain all our lives to become *grown up*, or *mature*. By the time we reach forty, we sense vaguely that there are parts of us still waiting to grow up. Not surprisingly, we see immaturity more clearly in other people than we do in ourselves. At the same time, we notice that we do not have the energy of our younger years, saying, half facetiously, that it is the tribulations of life that eat away at our strength, or that "gray hair is hereditary; we get it from our children."

Only in more recent times have we come to accept the idea that the child in us is a plus, not a minus. With the advent of "reality" therapy, the "child" has come to have equal importance with the "adult" and the "parent."

We knew that all along, as we "gave in" to childish pleasures or exhibited childish exuberance, albeit with disclaimers about "not being grown-up yet." But not until we are confronted with a situation in our own lives can we fully understand the importance of the child or what it means in everyday events or at times of crises.

Jesus understood it when he said,

Whoever does not receive the Kingdom of God like a child shall not enter it.

MARK 10:15

One of the best examples is one of the most common.

Your friend is a very special person with whom you share everything, even your most personal secrets. One day when you call her she seems to be distant, cold. She says she will call you back, but she doesn't. The next day you think about calling her but decide that maybe her coldness was due to some breakdown in the relationship. Maybe she is angry with you about something. You put off calling, feeling worse as time goes by. Then you begin to wonder, could it be that she doesn't like you any more?

Chances are, you discover later that she had something on her mind, completely unrelated to you, and you let it drop, forgetting the incident. But it points up something important. Our first reaction is to wonder, "Maybe she doesn't love me any more." Is the other person withdrawing his or her love from us?

When that happens, we are suddenly transported back to the age of three, or five, or whatever period it was in our life when we were learning what love looked like from our father or mother. Needing acceptance of ourselves as persons of worth starts from the day we are born and never stops. It is a crucial part of our faith.

When Mother scolded us, our first reaction was fear, that it meant she didn't love us. When Father frowned, we wondered if it meant he didn't love us. And when Mother or Father were unable to balance punishment or discipline with touching and caring, the child came to believe that he must not be worth loving, or else surely Mother or Father would hug or kiss them, or speak loving words.

The world is full of grown-up children whose mothers and

fathers were unable or unwilling to express caring in terms that the child could translate as "love." They often are angry, hurt, resentful adults, wondering if the failure of a friend to respond as expected means the friend doesn't love them either. Unless a child learns to love himself by experiencing the caring respect of the parent, he may never, or only with great difficulty, discover how to love another human. If a person is unable to love, faith in God's love never becomes a reality.

Paul said that there came a time when we should

> *not be children any longer, tossed to and fro . . .*
>
> *Rather speaking the truth in love,*
> *may grow up in every way into him*
> *who is the head, into Christ.*
>
> EPHESIANS 4:14-15

Through the centuries religions have recognized the need to believe that we are loved, and much time is spent talking about "God loves you," or "Jesus loves me." Many religious groups believe that there must come a specific moment when we accept that love and can, therefore, turn away from our unloving ways. It is called conversion. Religions have recognized that we can be loving only if we are loved. There have been thousands of books written and thousands and thousands of articles, discussions, and seminars, all trying to figure out how to "convert" people, how to bring them to the understanding that God loves them.

We all know children who seem to need more love than the other children in the family, who never seem to have enough.

A friend of mine has three children, two of whom have moved into adulthood with an adequate sense of personal worth. But Mike has never believed that anyone loved him, not really, and certainly not God. Now twenty-seven, he has been married three times, looking for love through another person and not finding it.

That family, including the other children, did everything they could think of to let Mike know he was loved, but he never believed it. Whenever they did loving, even sacrificial, things for him, he rejected the offering. It was as if he was saying, "You don't really love me; you are just pretending in order to make me feel good." And, of course, that is exactly what they were doing, trying to give him a feeling of acceptance and love so that he could love himself, not as a pretense, but because they did truly love him as their child and brother.

Recently I was watching my daughter nursing her two-month old baby. The baby's eyes were fastened on his mother's face as he nursed and as she talked to him in loving words, tones and touches. I envisioned in my mind the baby's father walking in and saying something angry to the mother, and the mother's angry or frightened response. The mother's tender words and touch would be replaced by tension and anger, conveyed through her tightened muscles and voice tone change. The baby would have no way of knowing the anger was not directed toward him. That tiny child would learn very early about the relationship between his father and mother and their relationship to him. The most important gift a father can give his child is to love the child's mother and show it.

No one seems to know exactly how we come to the realization and the acceptance that we are loved, but it does seem to rise out of our early years.

My own lesson in this came because I had to find answers at a time of crisis.

For years I tried to discuss our relationship with my husband and was usually met with silence, or at best, mono-syllables. The pressure would build, and finally I would blow up, reinforcing John's feeling that I "intimidated" him with my anger, which sent him back into silence.

At a conference away from home I learned from friends that John wanted a divorce and was committed to marry another woman. My anger was intense, but, although a confrontation was obviously necessary, I dreaded it, fearful that it would again result in a blow-up, anger, and only negative results.

Expecting John to announce his demand for a divorce immediately upon my arrival home from the conference, I was surprised when he said nothing, and it was a measure of my own intimidation that I too said nothing. Fortunately I was scheduled for a meeting with my counselor the next morning. It went like this:

Counselor: What do we need to work on today? What is happening?

I: I am very angry. I learned from friends that John wants a divorce and that he is going to marry another woman. Yet I have been home for twenty-four hours, and he has said nothing to me! I want to confront him but I am afraid I will scream at him and blow him away.

Counselor: I hear you saying that you are angry, but I feel you saying you are hurt.

I: That's right, I am hurt that he let me find out from someone else, but I never learned how to handle my anger with the men in my life. My father never gave me a role model for that.

Counselor: Tell me about your father.

I: I was never close to him; I was afraid of him.

Counselor: Let's do something here. Close your eyes and try to recall the first time you remember being angry with your father, when you were eight or nine. Now it may take a few minutes. Just relax and . . .

I: No. I don't need a few minutes. I remember it well . . .

Counselor: All right, you are there. Describe the scene to me. Use the present tense.

I: I am in the barn with my father. He has just beaten my dog and I scream at him, "I hate you!"

Counselor: Say that again.

I: I hate you!

Counselor: What did your father do?

I: He shouted at me, "Get the hell to the house!"

And suddenly, in the counselor's office, I was crying, my face in my hands. Sobbing, pulling the forty-year-old pain from deep within myself, on and on I cried.

Finally the tears subsided.

Counselor: You have come to the house and your father has just come in the door. What do you want to say to him?

I: Why did you beat my dog? If you loved me, you wouldn't beat my dog.

The counselor got up and moved; then motioning to a chair, he resumed the dialogue:

Counselor: Sit in this chair. It is your father's chair. What would you want your father to say to you?

I: I loved you, but I didn't know how to show it.

Counselor: Say that again.

I: I loved you, but I didn't know how to show it.

We were quiet for a few moments. Then the counselor spoke. "As you were talking, your hands were clenched in anger, but what was really going on was that you were hurt, deeply hurt. When you were eight years old, you needed that anger to protect you from your father, but you don't need that anger any more. What you need now is to be able to show John that you are hurting. When you shout at him, all he sees is your angry face."

"That's right," I said, "I need to tell him that I am hurting, instead of shouting at him."

"Can you do that?"

"Yes . . . yes, I can do that."

What a lesson! And it was doubly reinforced that week when, once as I was looking at my husband, instead of his face, I saw my father's face. In the past, each time my husband had become angry and refused to talk to me, I had seen my father's angry face, and the hurt had welled up, causing me to shout in angry tones, unaware that my primary emotion was pain, not anger.

I was a little eight-year-old girl, when, fearful that my father did not love me, I shouted in fright, and again, later, when I shouted at my husband, fearful that his silent anger indicated that he, too, was withdrawing his love from me. I was returning to the most basic fear of all humans, the fear of loss of love.

It was no different for John. In my face he saw the angry

face of his mother and assumed that if I loved him, I would not shout at him.

I learned my lesson too late to save my marriage, but not too late to change a myriad of other relationships, to rediscover the meaning of God's love.

A few months later I made a journey to my childhood home, where I told my father about my new understanding. It was a freeing experience for him, for he had always sensed my reticence, but was unable to bridge the gap of all those years. When I was ready to board my plane, he kissed me for the first time in my memory.

When my daughter declines an invitation to come to supper, the fleeting thought could go through my mind, "Have I done something wrong; does this mean she doesn't love me as much as she used to?" But instead, I accept her explanation of other commitments and go my way.

When I have prepared supper and my son declines even a taste, I could take that as a personal rejection, since, after all, I went to that trouble just for him. Instead, I accept his explanation that he is just not hungry.

We are at all times, three and thirty-three, five and fifty-five. How beautiful that we can tap into the child-like joy and wonder, but we must be aware that we also retain the fear and pain of those early relationships. The meaning of God's love comes to us when we discover meaning in other relationships.

How much energy we expend in fretting about situations like these, when we could free ourselves to give all our attention to

> grow up in every way into Christ,
> from whom the whole body, joined and knit together,
> when each part is working properly,
> makes bodily growth and upbuilds itself in love

> EPHESIANS 4:16

The body that is growing and working properly will have the energy needed to grow and love.

chapter eight

Celebrate the Pain

I always thought "celebrate" meant a happy occasion. Now I know that it can be an event of extreme pain but one that can bring healing.

I found myself going through the estrangement of a separation and probable divorce. Oh, I was going to do it the mature way! I would never lose control; everyone would know how brave and courageous I was.

Then the reality of what was happening to me suddenly hit like a ton of bricks. John was leaving; he wasn't coming back. After more than thirty years with the same man in my bed and at the breakfast table, my marriage was ending.

How could I be calm and courageous? My world was falling into pieces even as I watched.

Feeling responsible for half of what went wrong in the marriage, I wanted us to go to a counselor and work on the relationship. But John decided not to stay to try to change things.

I was in pain, terrible pain. The distress began showing up in physical symptoms—headache, heartburn, muscle spasms, loss of appetite, loss of sleep, diarrhea. I tried to lay the blame on other things, but I understood my body well enough to know that it was reacting to a life-threatening experience. I was going to have to do something!

My pastor said we should celebrate the beginnings and endings of our lives. This was an ending. Later, I could hope to celebrate the beginning of a new life, but now it was definitely an ending.

We forget too easily that, for the disciples, the Last Supper Jesus had prepared was the celebration of an ending and the intimation of a beginning. On Friday it was "my body broken and blood shed for you"; on Sunday, it was my body and blood renewed and resurrected.

All right, then, I told myself, if this cup could not be removed, if it could not be pushed aside or ignored, I would go right through the middle of it. I would immerse myself in it and celebrate it.

I sat down and thought about that. To celebrate means to hold up an event and take from it whatever gifts it has for us. If the gift is joy, then we enjoy the pleasure. If the gift is anger, then we recognize it and use the energy from the anger to do something about what made us angry. If it is pain from a wound, we accept it so we can move on to healing.

When that realization came to me, I was sitting in my living room staring at the fire, wondering if I could take more aspirin; it had been only two hours since the last ones. Instead of deadening the pain, I laid it out in front of me.

Aloud, I described my feelings of rejection, the loneliness of separation, the brokeness of the relationship, my fear of no financial support, my terrible sense of failure to accomplish the loving marriage I wanted.

Tears flowed unchecked. On and on I cried.

Finally I dropped into bed, exhausted. The next morning the edge was off the misery and the headache was gone.

I cried again and again, but each time I held nothing back.

After all, my whole body and psyche were in crisis. Why pretend this was not a "life-threatening" situation? To fail to admit the gravity of the threat to my emotional stability would have postponed the healing, maybe forever.

My anguish was associated with specific facts of my life, but the emotion covered them up. Dealing with the pain allowed me to get beneath to the problem.

One by one I tackled the problems that were causing my pain, letting the feelings wash over me. Each time I came out with a new perspective on the problem and with renewed strength to work at it. And more than that, my physical symptoms were shortlived.

When someone asked, "How are you?" I didn't try to hide what was going on in my life. I said, "I'm all right. I'm in pain, but I'm all right." It was true.

That was the message of the Lord's Supper. Instead of running away, Jesus chose to celebrate his fear and pain to find meaning in them and thereby gather the will-power to see them through.

I looked around and saw friends who had gone through divorce or other life accidents, carrying around open wounds but refusing to admit they were suffering. Two of them were still angry, bitter people several years after the event.

There are many ways to celebrate pain, anger or fear to control or transform it. One effective method is to cut out pictures from a magazine that express some of what you are feeling. Tape them to your bathroom mirror or a frequently-used door. By the time you realize you are no longer noticing them, the emotion will have been resolved.

A person out of touch with his emotions may have to use other people's words. If expressing feelings is difficult for you, read poetry or the Bible to find ways of putting your feelings into words.

Having someone else who is as frightened as you can make being alive a true celebration. But sometimes that other person may not be available? What else can you do?

Reading the Psalms can effectively give expression to a

gamut of emotions. But an even more effective way to celebrate what is going on inside of you is to write your own Psalm. Read a few out of the Bible and then pour out your heart on paper.

My "Psalm for a Day of Agony" came out of just such a need to express my feelings:

O Lord, my friend is tired of hearing of my pain,
　　　But so am I!
How long can this go on
　　　before I collapse under the burden?
In fact, even now I see myself
　　　sprawled under the weight of my sin and misjudgments.
Only my feet and arms extend out,
　　　and they are flailing the air,
　　　trying to right my soul again.

I am so frightened!
　　　Where will the money come from?
　　　How will I be able to repair the roof?
　　　How can I stand being alone the rest of my life?
　　　What if I don't know enough about the God within me?
And I am still angry,
　　　Angry at him,
　　　　　for rejecting me after all these years,
　　　　　for not being the person he could have been.
　　　Angry at myself,
　　　　　for settling for so small a vision of marriage,
　　　　　for expecting more of him that I had a right to expect.

But I rejoice . . .
　　　That You have never been far from me,
　　　That You have entered my consciousness whenever
　　　　　I would allow it,
　　　　　And spoke to me.
　　　That the tulips are going to bloom
　　　　　And the roses are going to live.
Don't let me give up now, God.
　　　I've come so far!
　　　So far from where I was so few months ago.

Don't let me slip back now, God,
I like me better this way.

But I have so far to go,
And I have to go it alone.

Stay near, God!
Please!

Then I began reading about myself. In *Psychology Today*, a psychotherapist said, "It seemed that when people allowed themselves to experience the full emotional impact of a critical life situation, physical symptoms were much less likely to arise. By contrast, people who did not fully experience the pain of a difficult event were much more prone to physical symptoms. If they did not cry, rage, call for help, or remember painful events, their bodies seemed to do those things for them."[10]

"My God, my God, why . . . . ?" cried Jesus from the cross. And through his rage and pain, he could confidently say, "Father, into thy hands I commit my spirit."

In the *Aquarian Conspiracy*, the author says, "Pain no longer intimidates us as we begin to reap the rewards of its resolution. Each survival and transcendence gives courage for the next encounter. The survivor knows the truth of Viktor Frankl's statement, 'What is to give light must endure burning.'

"Fear of giving up any part of our current life inventory vanishes as we realize that all change is by choice. *We drop only what we no longer want.* Fear of self-inquiry is overcome because the self turns out to be not the dark, impulsive secret we had been warned about but a strong, sane center."[11]

In John 10, Jesus said, "For this reason the Father loves me, because I lay down my life, that I may take it again," implying a reluctance to yield to the lessons of pain. But he insists, "No one takes it from me, but I lay it down of my own accord. I have power to lay it down, and I have power to take it again; this charge I have received from my Father."

To take charge of our lives, to accept the pain that comes packaged with living, is to lay hold of the power necessary for victorious living, to be assured that "the Father loves me."

After that "life accident" was over, I decided to never stop celebrating whatever is going on in my life at that moment, to immerse myself in it. Joy, love, anger, pain: Each one is an honest emotion that is vital to my growth into the resurrection that I am celebrating today.

chapter nine

You Have a Responsibility to Be Angry

Since we are taught from childhood not to demonstrate angry feelings, we more often than not hide them, fastening them onto some part of our body. The stomach, the digestive system, the kidneys, the heart, all become victims of suppressed emotions, with anger leading the list. Notorious for leaving us shaken and drained, anger is something we need to look at in the light of our faith commitment.

> *Listen to me, God!*
> *and don't hide from my begging!*
> *Stay with me!*
> *Answer me!*
> *I am really upset!*
>
> PSALM 55:1-2

Jumping up, Donald stomped to the front door and slammed it behind him as he left. Joyce sat, dumbfounded. It was the first time in their twenty-three-year marriage that he had lost control like that. It was not the result she had predicted when, earlier that day, she had decided *something* had to be done to change the pattern of their relationship.

In discussions about their marriage, Donald would always remain mostly silent, contributing to the conversation only a few words or sentences. Normally a calm person under stress, Joyce would finally blow up, shouting at times.

She never felt good after those outbursts. Her anger was not assuaged; the situation was not improved; the pattern of her wrath and his silence was reinforced.

Donald was to come that afternoon to discuss the financial settlement for the divorce, definitely an emotionally-charged situation.

As Joyce passed her desk she noticed a magazine with the story of a man who had worked for peace all his life. A co-worker said to him, "You have seen death and destruction and pain, and yet you are a happy man. How can this be?"

The man replied, "It is because I am so angry. There are things in our world that I should be angry about—hunger, war, destructive governments; I have a right to be angry. But I use the energy that comes from the anger to do something about what is making me angry."

That was it! That was the answer Joyce had been looking for. The energy from her anger that came out in shouting because he would not answer had given Donald an excuse for continuing to remain silent. Obviously when Joyce began to shout, she "lost"; by remaining quiet, apparently in control of himself, Donald always "won." The relationship would never get anywhere as long as that destructive pattern of her resentment and Donald's silence continued.

This time, Joyce told herself, she would use the energy to prepare herself for the talks of the afternoon. She set about getting together all the facts she would need.

In the middle of it Joyce had to run an errand and happened to meet a woman whom she normally avoided. The woman had a way of arousing irritation in Joyce, and since Joyce had always

72

had the idea that any show of anger was bad, maybe even un-Christian, the answer was to avoid her. That day she decided to try out her new pattern.

Joyce said something to the woman about a project they were both involved in, carefully stating her point. Clearly, the woman was surprised that Joyce would converse with her. She replied testily, and Joyce quietly restated her point. The woman left, obviously upset, not knowing how to handle the situation.

As she thought about it, Joyce realized that the woman didn't know what to do since the rules of the game they were playing seemed to have changed. Joyce had initiated new rules by speaking directly to her instead of avoiding her, and by speaking calmly and with assurance instead of angrily, as was expected.

That positive experience gave Joyce encouragement, and when Donald arrived that afternoon, she invited him to sit down at the kitchen table, where she showed him the facts and figures and explained the rationale for her proposal. For an hour-and-a-half they talked. At no time did she raise her voice, but neither did she back off. Donald did talk more than usual, since she was willing to wait for long periods for an answer. He became more and more agitated and finally leaped up and stomped out of the front door, shouting at her and slamming the door behind him.

What a surprise! Joyce would never have predicted such a response, but decided it was probably for the same reason the woman that morning had walked away in a huff. The rules they had always played by had been changed. Donald could no longer have the excuse of her displeasure to retreat into silence, and when he found her prepared with clear facts and figures, he could not handle it.

The next time they got together, exactly the same thing happened, and he again left in a rage.

Joyce found that using the energy from her anger to prepare her case and then presenting it with calm and confidence did more than the shouting to accomplish the goals she had in mind. After being frustrated to the point of shouting, she had a feeling of powerlessness, not control. While presenting her case with calm, she felt very much in control of herself and of the situation. And when it was over, she was not worn out from the emotional trauma. Feeling good about herself, having faith that she could handle the situation with integrity, gave her a control and a calmness unknown before. Each success reinforced her good feelings about her ability to handle difficult situations.

Many times, anger masks fear, and we shout to cover up our fright, for to admit it is to make ourselves vulnerable. As our love becomes more nearly perfect, our fear proportionately diminishes, for "perfect love casts out fear."

James (1:20) says everyone should be "quick to hear, slow to speak, slow to anger, for anger does not work the righteousness of God."

There is an interesting phenomenon that takes place in anger. When you find a way to deal with the resentment you are feeling toward someone close, you may discover that negative feelings you have about other people in your life begin to fade. It is as if one must justify the other, or that anger at one becomes anger at others.

But when anger is preventing us from doing what is necessary, it is helpful to know what to do about that anger; the need is real and immediate.

In the book *Pathfinders*, the author says, "The person who routinely ignores the uncomfortable emotions that signal the need to change himself is a person refusing to risk the next stage of development.

"Somatization—the translation of emotional ills a person is afraid to express to one of the body's organs—is one sure signal of the need to risk change. We humans are infuriatingly creative at finding ways to avoid risking change."[12]

In the last chapter we talked about "celebrating" emotions that rise up within us. "Celebrating" anger is one of the best ways to deal with it.

Going over the specific details of the event is part of that experience, not for the purpose of savoring the vexation rising from it, but to clarify exactly what happened. This can be done in silence, aloud, or by writing it down.

I have found a very effective method of defusing negative

emotions. After writing down all I feel and all I remember about the situation, I then write a letter to the person I am angry with. Then going back over the pages, line by line, I say to myself, "I'm going to forget that—and that—and that."

One by one I mark out the lines.

A more graphic way is to use a computer with word processing software. After typing the list of grievances, you pick out the ones you can forget first, push the delete button, and watch them disappear. Then move on to the tougher ones. There is something about watching the words disappear and then surveying the empty page that assists the mind in actually erasing the anger. The experience is a rite of celebration, a cathartic one.

If, when I am finished, there are still some lines left undeleted, I decide whether or not to put it away until tomorrow or to go ahead with conflict resolution as outlined in Chapter 17. Sometimes confrontation is the only way to resolve the situation.

The difference between men's and women's responses under stress are worth noting.

Women tend to accept guilt for whatever is going wrong in their lives; their children's bad grades or unkempt rooms, their husband's unhappiness, their own failures. Men tend to find a reason outside themselves and fasten onto it as the cause of their trouble, as their "enemy."

Finding ways to live out our faith in the difficult days of this rapidly-changing society includes finding ways to deal with anger. Society has taught Americans that showing anger is definitely unacceptable, but there *is* a time to be angry.

Jesus, in the temple, was angry when unprotected people were being hurt, when the temple rulers were not following the Micah commandment to

Do justice, and to love kindness and to
walk humbly with your God

MICAH 6:8

The problems of the world are so huge and so complex that there seems to be little we can do about them. Children go to bed hungry and cold every night; families are uprooted, living in lean-tos as a result of war; fathers or brothers disappear, victims of oppressive governments, leaving mothers and children to fend for themselves.

More and more women are finding themselves alone, without financial resources, as a result of the death of their husbands or divorce. Because most of those in need are women, poverty is becoming "feminized." To be left with money enough to pay only the minimum bills is frightening and often results in anger.

> *A voice was heard in Ramah,*
> *wailing and loud lamentation,*
> *Rachel weeping for her children;*
> *she refused to be consoled,*
> *because they were no more*
>
> MATTHEW 2:18

In the face of such pain and loss, we see little hope.

Where is the hope that comes from faith? Instead of hope, we are often immersed in despair about our inability to do anything about the world's problems. Despair drains our energy as we flail at the causes of the problems.

All of these evidences of "man's inhumanity to man" should make us very angry. Not only do we have a right to be angry, we have a responsibility to be angry, to use that energy to do something about what makes us angry. Only then will our faith be renewed, faith in ourselves and our ability to relieve suffering—ours as well as that of others.

chapter ten

The Mansion of Many Rooms

As we learn to celebrate and conquer each problem and fear, our faith is strengthened by each experience, and we may think that we will eventually rid ourselves of all major problems. Ah, but that is not to be so, for things that are alive never stop changing and growing. Every time we close one door, another opens behind it.

A door of Paul's life banged shut behind him, never to open again, when he was struck blind on the road to Damascus. As a result, Paul entered a new way of life that took him into many dangerous main streets and alleys, and finally to his death.

At Mysia, Paul ran into the tightly shut door that led to Bithynia and walked instead through the door to Troas, where he had the vision of the man of Macedonia calling to him. This event opened up a whole new arena for him.

For a year I stumbled half-blind through the house that was my life, opening one door after another, surprised and grateful that I somehow managed to make it through one room after another.

In the first room I was forced to share my pain; in the second room I set a goal that would never be out of my sight. In another room I learned to "celebrate" the ending of a relationship, and I discovered how to use anger constructively.

One lesson after another was written on my slate as I moved from one classroom to the next in the university of life.

After a while I became bone-weary, wondering when it would end. Scars covered my body and psyche. Surely I would come to the end of the course before long!

Then the truth began to dawn on me. It was not that a new problem arose every time I managed to get one under control; the problems had always been there, hidden by the other ones, waiting to be uncovered.

Each time I opened the door to a room where a problem lay in wait, I tackled the problem and worked my way through it. With relief, I would stand erect, tired but triumphant over the problem, only to see before me a door, standing ajar, leading into another room—and the only way out was through that next room.

Each problem was only one room of many in the huge mansion that is my life. Each one was connected to the one before it and the one that came after, but one problem could not be tackled until the one in the room before it was solved. Once I understood that, I no longer expected each problem to be the last one. In fact, I even wondered what it would be like to have to stay in the room where I was forever. In each room I met interesting people from whom I learned important lessons, and I came to look forward to what would surely be an adventure in the next room.

Another image presents itself in this age of the computer. As you work at the computer, you push the various keys necessary for working through whatever problem is at hand. Finally, you touch the key that will draw it all together and finish it off, and there you are, with an empty screen in front of you and a whole new problem to be solved, a new story to be written. It never ends.

There were times when I wanted to turn and run away. Did I really need to resolve this problem? I didn't even know how. What if the answer was one I didn't want? What if I could not find the answer by myself? And what if . . .?

Sometimes the answer to the problem is so difficult that you would almost rather live with the problem.

Moses had had it! The people of Israel, wandering in the wilderness, were supplied with manna, which they fried, boiled, stewed, baked, and made into little cakes. No doubt some woman in the camp compiled all the recipes for using manna and became the "manna expert." But they were sick of manna . . . and Moses was sick of their complaining about it. He and God had some sharp words.

"Why did you do this to me?" Moses demanded. "Why did you make me take on the burden of all these people? Did I conceive them that you should tell me to 'Carry them in your bosom as a nurse carries the sucking child?' Where am I to get the meat they are crying for?"

Then Moses' lamentations became more profound: "I'm not able to carry these people alone; the burden is too heavy for me. If you treat me this way, kill me at once, so that I will not have to look at my wretchedness."

God answered Moses, telling him to follow certain orders, saying, "Tell the people to get ready, for tomorrow they shall eat meat."

But even then Moses was skeptical. "There are six hundred thousand people here, and you say, 'I will give them meat!' Where is all this meat going to come from?" And Moses became sarcastic. "Are all the fish of the sea going to be brought here for them to eat?"

But God didn't lose patience, and merely said, "Watch and see."

The next day huge flocks of quail appeared.

Perhaps Moses thought the problem was solved, the door closed, but not so. Another problem appeared; the people became gluttonous and wasted the meat, which made God very upset.

The saga of the Israelites wandering in the desert is the

story of doors opening and closing on one challenge after another. It is our story too.

Carol lost her husband suddenly, tragically. Their finances were minimal; she would need to go to work immediately. But with two small children, her options were limited. Before the children were born she had been a secretary with considerable skill in many areas of copy preparation and writing. Living near a college gave her access to customers who would need help with manuscript writing and typing, but she needed a word processor/computer.

After many hours of checking out models, makes, and features, she decided which one would be best for the job at a price that was reasonable, but it would mean asking the bank for a loan. That struck terror into her heart, and she backed off, going back to reading the want ads.

One day she was talking with a friend and admitted her fear of banks and bankers. "Of course," Carol said, "they won't let me borrow money with what little security I have."

Her friend said, "The answer is always 'no' until you ask. It may still be 'no' then, but then again, it may be 'yes.' But it is *always* 'no' until you ask."

"Of course!" Carol said. "The worst they can do is refuse, and I won't be any worse off than I am now."

Then her friend showed her how to write a proposal for the bank, showing just what she had in mind, what her assets were and why she thought she would be able to make the payments. One of the assets she listed was "exceptional secretarial expertise."

The next morning Carol dressed in her best suit and confident smile and went to the bank.

When the interview was over and the money was in Carol's account, the loan officer, a woman, said, "Your most important asset is your confidence. It will take you a long way toward success."

Carol smiled and thanked her, grateful for a lesson learned about the answer being "no" until you ask.

Jesus told the father of the epileptic, "All things are possible to him who believes." God does not expect us to sit around

80

waiting for Him to take care of our needs. Having the courage to believe in the face of unbelief is what faith looks like. The father replied to Jesus, "I believe; help my unbelief!"

But, sometimes it seems as if there just aren't any satisfactory answers.

Rachel had gone though one room after another, each one at a lower level than the one before, until one night she found herself in a room without windows, light, or hope. The problem in this room was too overwhelming. Her resources were used up, gone, she couldn't cope any longer. Her body was so tired, so very tired. She gave herself to utter despair. Life was too much; death seemed preferable. Yes—death was a better choice.

She prepared to end her life.

As she stood on the dividing line between this world and the next, ready to administer the fatal dose, she became aware of something, or someone, inside herself—and yet separate from herself. That something reached out and pulled her back from the brink, back into her world.

Exhausted, she fell into bed and slept, waking the next morning, remembering that something, or someone, had pulled her back. It had not come from outside herself, but from within. It was part of her, and yet "she, herself" would have taken her life.

Suddenly the truth broke over her. That "savior" was part of her, and yet separate from her, a power present within her from the beginning, part of the eternal and of eternity, but appearing only when it seemed she was no longer able to make the choice of life.

What a discovery! Jesus said it clearly: "The Kingdom of God is within you."

There was something powerful enough to get through to her in a moment of highest stress that cared enough about her to save her, that was security of the most solid kind. And it was right there within her!

She would never be afraid again! This something from out of eternity would surely go with her into the realm of death, so

Rachel knew with certainty that she would never be afraid of death. But more important, far more important, was the understanding that she would never be afraid to live! With that kind of Being always present, even the most difficult problems could be handled. For this was surely God speaking to her! She had experienced God as surely as if she had seen him.

It was her moment of transformation from a frightened, discouraged, weary woman into a woman of hope, with faith in the future and renewed energy to face her problems.

Job understood it, too:

> *I had heard of thee by the hearing of the ear,*
> > *But now my eye sees thee.*
> *And the Lord blessed the latter days of Job more than his beginning.*

For those of us in our mid-years, the problems to be faced are very different from those of our children. Add to that the belief that we are in a major moment of transformation as a human culture on the earth, and one can understand the dilemma of young people as well as that of their parents in trying to understand what is happening to their children.

The answers to "How are your children doing?" may be:

"One is married, unmarried. (Divorced)

Another is unmarried, married. (Living with her 'significant other.')

The other is married, married. (Married.)"

The trauma of watching our children trying to cope with their world leaves many parents dependent on coffee, alcohol, or other drugs to overcome their feelings of helplessness, weariness, and hopelessness.

Today's young people have many decisions to make. For most young people growing up in middle class America in the 1940's, there were some questions that were never asked:

† Shall I go to church?
  Of course, we went to church. Didn't everyone? That's where you met your friends.

† Shall I go to college?
College was the doorway to a profession and financial security, the American Dream. Everyone went if it was humanly possible.

† Shall I marry or live with him/her?
Of course, we married. Living together was immoral, wasn't it?

† Shall I marry at all?
There was almost no alternative for a young woman. Marriage, and children, was her destiny. And a man must have a family for which he would bring home the paycheck.

† Shall I be heterosexual or homosexual?
Neither word was spoken aloud in polite society. Homosexuals didn't exist, for all practical purposes.

† Shall we have children?
Who had a choice? That was before the day of the pill.

† Shall the young man get a job?
No one, but *no one*, thought not working was a viable option. How would you pay the bills?

† Shall we stay married or get a divorce?
Divorce was not an option except in cases so rare as to be only gossip, and then the woman remarried immediately, for of course, she had no way to support herself.

Now, not only do young people have these choices, but they cannot escape making them! To not decide, is to decide.

A woman may not refuse to decide about birth control, for it will result in children which she may or may not be able to support and care for, with or without a husband/father.

"Living together" is considered "marriage" in many states, making a "divorce" necessary if the couple breaks up.

To not get a job is to trigger other forces that impinge on young people's decisions.

There was a time when we thought the American Dream would become a reality. When, after the struggle for financial security, and after the children were raised, we would have reached the End of the Rainbow, and achieved our goal of becoming the Perfect parents of perfect children in a society where everyone had plenty and "justice would roll down like the ocean."

Alas, whether in personal, community, or national terms, we discovered that every time we walked into a room, worked on the problem there, and were ready to move on, there was another room, another problem, another challenge to our faith, another drain on our energies.

It will ever be so, but that is at once a bane and a blessing. How uninteresting to think that all the problems might be solved, for it is in the Darkness that we meet God. It is in the meeting of God, in the challenge of finding the answers to the problems in each room, that we find the recurring joy of being alive, for our faith has told us, "This too shall pass."

Someday I will open the last door and walk through it, but until then, I will never stop wondering who and what I will find in the next room that, although traumatic, may enrich my life and enlarge my understanding. To step into the next room with hope is part of faith. To refuse that encounter is to refuse to meet God.

> *Even though I walk through the*
>> *valley of the shadow of death,*
> *I fear no evil;*
>>> *for thou art with me;*
>>> *thy rod and thy staff,*
>>> *they comfort me.*

chapter eleven

Healing Through Pain

The law of the Lord is perfect,
reviving the soul

PSALM 19:7

Both of my arms were numb! Then, as feeling ebbed back into my fingers, the throbbing pains began. The slightest movement sent electric shocks through my arms.

Thank goodness it was the day of my appointment with the neurologist. This was serious!

To my amazement the doctor found nothing. He only made me very angry by saying that there was no neurological explanation for the entire arm going numb.

What did he mean by "no neurological explanation"?

"Well," he said, "the nerve patterns in the arms do not allow for the entire arm going to sleep like that. Pressure on the nerve at the elbow would cause numbness of part of the hand.

Other nerves could be pinched and cause other anesthesias, but not all at the same time."

Then what was causing my arms to go to sleep? He had no explanation.

I didn't have a very high opinion of that neurologist. A specialist ought to be able to give me some relief.

I wore foam rubber pads on my elbows at night, slept propped up in bed, or didn't sleep at all.

Meanwhile, my preparations for a three-week trip to Europe with my daughter were complete. My husband was not going, and as the trip drew nearer, I felt more troubled about leaving him behind. Also, having traveled before, I knew the strain of jet lag, strange foods, and foreign ways.

I developed heartburn which became more severe as the time came to leave. That did not come as a surprise; experience had shown that heartburn was one way my body told me it was under stress. When the stress was gone, the heartburn also disappeared.

We arrived in France, and suddenly the heartburn disappeared. Apparently the strain related to leaving home was gone, so the heartburn could go, too.

But to my amazement, the numbness in my arms also disappeared completely, and did not return.

What possible explanation was there? Looking back, I realized that on the mornings when I wakened with numb arms, it was apparent that I had lain absolutely still, virtually without movement, the entire night, because of my tenseness. Holding those muscles tight over a long period of time resulted in the constriction of the nerves, putting my arms to sleep.

My body had found a new way to react to the stress I put on it. In addition to heartburn and headache, the stress could now put my arms to sleep.

From that experience I began to discover how to save doctor bills, and more importantly, I learned how to allow my body to help me cope with life's stresses.

I began to discuss more and more of my problems with God,

for I realized that without my covenant with Him, I would not have accepted the challenges that produced the stresses in my life. One without the other was impossible; I just needed to learn how to keep them in balance.

> *If the Lord had not been my help,*
> > *my soul would soon have dwelt in the land of silence*
> *When I thought, 'My foot slips,'*
> > *thy steadfast love, O Lord, held me up.*
> *When the cares of the heart are many,*
> > *thy consolations cheer my soul*

PSALM 94:17-19

Some months after the numbness episode I was preparing for the production of a play I had written. I was excited but fearful. Many, many hours had gone into the production. I had had little sleep, had eaten quick meals, and ran from one thing to another. The play was finally ready. It was a huge success. The next morning I stayed in bed, sick with a miserable cold.

This time I wasn't fooled. I had demanded extraordinary feats from my body, and it had come through . . . until it was all right for it to react, forcing me to give it the rest it needed.

Not long after that I agreed to accept a responsibility, which I immediately regretted. But I would not go back on my word. It involved working closely with someone who was extremely difficult to get along with.

One morning I wakened with a gripping pain in my right back. Presuming I had slept in a cramped position, I tried to forget it, but it would not be ignored. The pain became much worse. Finally I could not bear it any longer and made an appointment with the orthopedist for two days later.

The morning of the appointment I cancelled it; the job was finished and so was the backache.

My body had not appreciated the amount of stress I was putting on it and informed me that "what you are doing gives me a pain in the back!"

The Psalmist really understood what that was like:

Into thy hand I commit my spirit;
my eye is wasted from grief,
my soul and my body also.
For my life is spent with sorrow,
   and my years with sighing;
my strength fails because of my misery,
   and my bones waste away

PSALM 31:5, 9

One day my right jaw became numb. I know enough about my body to recognize serious symptoms. This was not just tension, I insisted. An internist looked me over and sent me to a dentist, a specialist in malocclusion of the mouth. After careful examination and x-rays, he sent me to a neurologist, who also took x-rays. The results? Nothing.

"Now wait a minute!" I said. "This is really serious!"

It became so bad that I could not chew without excruciating pain, and at times my jaw would slip out of joint.

Back to the dental specialist.

He said it was apparently a malocclusion, which would require considerable examination and probably grinding off of teeth. But he would not have an appointment opening for three weeks.

The next week marked the end of my responsibilities as chairperson of a group that had had many problems. The following week I cancelled the dental appointment; my mouth was back to normal and has remained so.

"All right, body," I said. "I've got your number. You aren't going to fool me any more. I understand that you will object to stress, and that's all right, but you aren't going to get all that attention from me. No more trips to specialists. Understand? The only medicine you are going to get from now on is more time spent in the 'desert', discovering what God has to say to me."

I took another trip to France, this time with my new daughter-in-law. We had signed up for language study in Paris, and I admitted to being scared to death to walk into that class made up of people from a dozen different countries of the world. No one but me spoke English!

Jet lag was causing some sleeping problems, but I had gone through such adjustments before. I could cope!

Three days later I was counting the days until it was time to go home. I had unbearable pain across my middle back. I told myself it had to be the bed, which was more like a hammock than a bed. Normally I refuse any kind of medication, but finally on the fourth day I took two aspirin, and the backache subsided. Relief, but only momentary. It returned with a vengeance. I started taking aspirin before the pain became unbearable and began thinking of how to find a doctor in France.

On Friday of the first week of my language study, the class took a test. I received a very high score, and when the teacher asked me a question in French, I was able to reply in French!

That night I slept free of pain and it did not return. My remaining two weeks in Paris were delightful.

From time to time the heartburn and headaches have reappeared, but I have not been taken in. I use aspirin or antacids if the pain is too severe, but I know that as soon as the situation clears up, the discomfort will leave too. And it does.

When I have seen other people in distress during tense times in their lives and suggested to them that their bodies might be reacting to stress, more often than not they became irate. Many of them spent much money trying to find a doctor who would cure them.

I assured them, "It's all right for the body to react, as long as you recognize the symptoms and know that when the stress is finished, the symptoms will leave also."

From those experiences, I now know some valuable facts about myself. Life is stressful; stress causes the body to react. The only way to prevent severe discomfort is to avoid tension, to remain uninvolved. But my life is exciting and full. I will not hibernate or hide from the risks that are necessary if I am going to enjoy life to its fullest.

Jesus said it clearly: "Therefore do not be anxious about tomorrow, for tomorrow will be anxious for itself. Let the day's own trouble be sufficient for the day."

A friend and I were discussing a mutual acquaintance, a young minister who had changed parishes recently.

"I heard just the other day that Bill had surgery for a herniated disc," I said.

My friend shook his head and said, "Bill is so determined to turn his congregation into a shining example of what a church ought to look like. He is trying to save the world, and he pushed his fears of failure into the muscles of his back. Finally they became so tense that they pulled his back out of alignment."

My friend went on, "The only obligation Bill has is to live up to his own personal covenant with God, having faith that God can take care of the church. Realizing that would have allowed his mind and body to relax."

Phillip kept going to see his doctor for diarrhea, assuming there was some physical reason for it. Then one day it dawned on him that every time he had a confrontation with his boss, within fifteen minutes, he had severe diarrhea. When he changed bosses, the diarrhea didn't return.

If you want to try a simple experiment to see if such a thing is possible, try this:

Think about someone you dislike very much. List three reasons why you dislike him; say them aloud. What happens to your stomach? Your back? Your neck? Each of us focuses our negative emotional energy on a certain part of our bodies. Doing this often enough will cause a headache, backache, or neck pain, possibly resulting in pathological changes if allowed to continue long enough.

Nadine found an excuse for what she saw as her continuing failures: allergies. After visiting specialists around the country, she could point to her latest allergy, holding a person's attention by reciting details in scientific terms. It gave her a sense of importance, for a little while. But inevitably, she had to return to the fact that she was unworthy, not as good as anyone else.

If only she could come to know that God loves her! Then she wouldn't have to make up illnesses as reasons for failure, since in God's eyes, she is already loved. But how does that transformation take place? It cannot be imposed from the outside; it must come from within.

Now, think about someone you love. List three reasons why you love that person; say them aloud. What happens to your stomach? Your back? Your head? No negative concentration of energy on parts of your body. Love brings relaxation and peace to our bodies because "perfect love casts out fear."

A special word, somatization, has been given to the syndrome that occurs when the emotional ills that we refuse to express are fastened onto a part of the body, such as the heart, the stomach, or the bowel. Leave the tension there long enough, it will cause irreversible changes in that organ. It is now believed that we may choose the kind of cancer we contract, depending on what kind of personality we possess. Pancreatic cancer is always accompanied by depression, but researchers are now beginning to think that depression possibly causes the cancer rather than the other way.

Once you have learned what stress does to your body, you are free to work your way through the stress, allowing your body the pain that goes with the challenge of living. You have a shield to protect you—the faith that God is with you.

Above all, take the shield of faith
EPHESIANS 6:16

If I accepted the symptoms as being physical in origin, they would remain while I sought cures. Heartburn could become an ulcer; back pain could become chronic arthritis; numbness could turn into perpetual loss of feeling. For there is no question but that prolonged conditions, from whatever cause, can result in permanent damage.

To recognize that your body develops symptoms in response to stress is not to admit weakness, but rather to be wise enough to allow your body to help you cope with your world.

In the Old Testament, putting a name on the Devil gave a person power over that devil. Mark tells the story of the man with an unclean spirit. "Jesus asked him, 'What is your name?' He replied, 'My name is Legion; for we are many'" Mark 5. Putting a name on the devils made it possible to control them.

Each time I discover the symptom my body has conjured up it is like putting a name on the devil. Then it no longer has control over me.

I wonder what new symptoms my body will think up. If it can cause numbness, pain, anesthesias, slipping of the jaws, it can find some others.

When your body complains, your first thought should not be to find a doctor who will give you a reason for your pain. You can accept the discomfort, if not with smiles, then at least with composure, for if you are attempting to live up to your covenant with God, stress is inevitable, even welcome.

> *Through him we have obtained access to this grace in which we stand, and we rejoice in our hope of sharing the glory of God. More than that, we rejoice in our sufferings, knowing that suffering produces endurance, and endurance produces character, and character produces hope, and hope does not disappoint us, because God's love has been poured into our hearts through the Holy Spirit which has been given to us*
>
> ROMANS 5:1-5

My ten-year-old son said, after reading his health book, "If we didn't have pain, we wouldn't know we needed to be healed."

It's true, healing does come through pain.

There is no better way to say it than Paul's words to the Philippians,

> *I can do all things through Christ which strengthens me*
>
> PHILIPPIANS 4:13

chapter twelve

We Are Tied to Our Source of Power

What is the nature of this "God"? What is our relationship to him that gives us strength when we need it?

That Sunday morning I wakened, and as always, did not open my eyes until I had assessed who I was and where I was in relation to my world.

There was a difference that morning. What was it? I opened my eyes and looked around. And I knew what it was.

I had come out of Intensive Care!

For six months I had been under round-the-clock care by three very dear friends who were on twenty-four call for me as I went through the throes of divorce. I no longer needed that kind of support. One by one I called them and said, "I am out of Intensive Care! I feel good—not great, but good!" And they each rejoiced in my healing.

Then I said to myself, "Now that you are no longer so intense, perhaps you should plan to set aside some time each day for prayer."

Prayer? I realized then that, as a matter of fact, I had been praying for six months, without ceasing, so close to the Ground of my Being, the God within me, that I was not even aware that I was talking to Her. (The God within me would surely be a woman.)

But that was too much, too intense. One could not maintain such a heavy relationship, for it had been to the exclusion of all other people. And as necessary as it was, for it was a matter of survival, I wanted to once again be involved in the lives and cares of the people around me.

My ability to pray without ceasing has not left, and now it is natural to slip in and out of prayer, often without my realizing it.

> *Pray constantly, give thanks in all circumstances, for this is the will of God in Christ Jesus for you.*
>
> I THESSALONIANS 5:17-18

Praying without ceasing means we live everyday as though God were everywhere present with us. A loved one gives us support even when absent, and when we are not consciously thinking of the person. It is the same with God.

Each person is defined by whatever relationship he has with the God within him. If his God is a loving, forgiving God, the person will be loving and forgiving, for that is what he understands he should be, God being the highest that we know and the goal we set for ourselves.

If his God is an angry, demanding Being, he will be fearful, always trying to please his God, making sacrifices. That kind of person is usually an angry individual, angry at God for demanding so much. The problem in this kind of relationship is that the human can never be good enough, never sacrifice enough, never work hard enough, to satisfy God, and he becomes angry because he senses that he will never satisfy this God. This person makes sacrifices for family, husband or wife and children, and when they do not seem to understand the measure of the sacrifice, he becomes angry at them too. He becomes a martyr.

Some people choose vocations that are more likely to support such a mind-set. Ministers and medical doctors head the list of people who tend to be martyrs since they are surrounded by parishioners and patients who reinforce their pattern. But it is an endless circle. The more they sacrifice, the more devotion they expect, but it is rarely enough to satisfy their need. Such vocations do not make people into martyrs; people who need that kind of life style go into those professions, which then confirm their beliefs about themselves.

Those persons do not understand that all of us are inadequate, none of us is good enough, and it is only by the Grace of God that we are forgiven. Even some pastors need to discover that God loves them!

Paul apparently understood this when he said in Ephesians (2:1-10)

> *But God, who is rich in mercy, out of the great love with which he loved us, even when we were dead through our trespasses, made us alive together with Christ (by grace you have been saved) and raised us up with him and made us sit with him in the heavenly places in Christ Jesus. For by grace you have been saved through faith; and this is not your own doing, it is the gift of God—not because of works, lest any man should boast.*

John Hunter, a pastor friend, described it very well. He said, "We are all on tethers, tied to our Source of Power. Some people are on short tethers; some on long. It takes more faith to be on a long tether, far from our Source of Power." Finding that an intriguing image, I have painted a picture of that scenario.

The people who are on short tethers are frightened, fearful people, afraid to move away because *they do not trust their Source of Power*, a power that could be called their "god." They fear that it will let them down, failing to be there when needed. At times, they become angry with their "god," for if only he were more dependable, they would be able to move out in faith and do so many good things in the world. As it is, they have undisputable reasons for failing; their god is too demanding, too uncaring. He keeps them tied in such a way that their range of movement is very limited.

"I have to work sixty hours a week; my family has to have the money."

"I can't take the children fishing; there's no one to answer my call."

"No vacation this year; I just can't get away."

Those may be excuses for doing what the person wanted to do anyway. Not surprisingly, a person like that gets angry if people do not appreciate his "sacrifice."

Everyone starts out on short ropes, but as some look ahead and see exciting challenges, they pull on the rope, stretching it, making it longer. The more they pull, the longer the rope and the farther they are from the Source of Power.

Those who are on long ropes often find themselves alone, for there aren't too many people out there in the far reaches. But the ones who are there are likely to be exciting, challenging, courageous people. The long tether permits a range of movement that is very wide, allowing for new and innovative endeavors.

And because they have faith in their Source of Power, they are joyous, free people. That is not to say they don't get angry with their "god" sometimes, when they suddenly need more rope and the only way to get it is to use their own strength to stretch the rope. It is easy to blame the Source of Power for the need to work harder than they would like to.

Have you ever been angry with your god?

The Psalmist was. In Psalm 77 he said:

> Will the Lord spurn forever
>> and never again be favorable?
> Has his steadfast love forever ceased?
>> Are his promises at an end for all time?
> Has God forgotten to be gracious?
>> Has he in anger shut up his compassion?

For a long time I assumed that the Source was God, the Creator. I said to a friend that, of course, God is that Source of Power. But she said, "The Source could be another person. My father was tied to my mother; she was his source of power, for he had never had a working relationship with God. When my mother was killed suddenly, he had no power of his own. That was twenty-five years ago, and since then, he has been almost a vegetable, contributing little to society, a tired man, his energy gone, afraid to live but more frightened of dying."

That led me to begin to look at people in a different way, and I have found many people who are tied in part or totally to another person. It is a safe place to be, for they can always blame the other person for not coming through when needed, all the time failing to realize that power does not come from another person but from within.

What better example of that than Adam who gave the classic excuse, "It was Eve who gave me the fruit of the tree," and Eve who said, "The snake fooled me." Neither would accept responsibility for his own life decision, giving away power instead of taking charge.

The need to acquire power through another person may help to explain in part the "unconditional love" syndrome that appears in second marriages, especially when the first marriage was of long duration, or the first spouse died. It seems to be more likely to happen to a man than to a woman.

When the man, who has remarried, becomes ill or runs into some major difficulty, he has an overwhelming need to return to the first mate, to the "unconditional love" that was born in the early days of their relationship. In spite of his being awkward, inexperienced, and poor, she had accepted him without reservation. Now he needs that total acceptance, a return to the Source of consolation, comfort, and strength. It is not unlike the Grace of God, but sought for in a human.

If that need is accompanied by guilt for having left the "unconditional love," it can destroy a second marriage.

The image we have of God comes from our early childhood experiences, usually with our fathers. Consequently, even women tend to have the concept of a male god. A friend of mine described to me what happened as she moved out of a dependent relationship with a man and into independence. "All my life the authority figures in my life had been men. When I married I merely transferred that authority to my husband. Then I accepted the responsibility for myself, in charge of my life. When the authority figure in my life became female, the God in my life became female also."

A contemporary Midwestern church congregation has, for three generations, been tied, not to God, in spite of being Christian, but to two strong families in the church. There is much mouthing of "God" words and talk of the "Lord," but their trust lies in the leaders who have, for all those years, told them what to do. The leaders fight among themselves for power, and the battles are "bloody," while the people who are tied to them stand by watching, unable to do anything but wring their hands and wish that peace would return and everyone would love each other again. There are the rich "ins," who are the leaders, and the poor "ins," who protect the family leaders against all comers, the "outs." It is not surprising that the current pastor gets caught in the middle of the fracas and leaves, having been blamed for the upset.

This kind of a group could be called a "battered congregation," not unlike a battered wife or battered child. The members expect to be told that they must sacrifice more, work harder, and support the leader families. The strange thing is that they have gone on, generation after generation, accepting their subservient role, believing that they are following "God." But all they really see are the figures of the leaders looming between them and God.

If the leaders are tied to God at all, it is with very short tethers, for they must find their "love" from the subject peoples in the congregation rather than from their relationship with God. Power over other people is a substitute for the love that should come from a right relationship with God.

The battered congregation members find the comfortable position as members of "family" to be more important than breaking away and following the God within them. Going against the "family" they are tied to is worse than living a spiritually-starved Life. Most important of all, they believe they deserve to be controlled, scolded, and "beaten," since "God" demands it. If they ever learned that God loves them, they would refuse to be in bondage to lesser beings.

Surrounding churches are now peopled with members of that congregation who valued their own ties with God and would not be intimidated by the leader families.

There is a simple, and historic, answer to such problems. What sets people of faith apart from others is that they have a covenant with God, each one of them, individually. They are, no doubt, participants in groups, but when there is a question of who is in charge, they merely refer to their covenant with God. So the question is not, "Whom shall we follow as our leader?" but rather, "What does being faithful look like at this moment?"

God's promise to the Israelites is as true for us today:

> For you are a people holy to the Lord your God; the Lord your God has chosen you to be a people for his own possession, out of all the peoples that are on the face of the earth. It was not because you were more in number . . . but it is because the Lord loves you, and is keeping the oath which he swore to your fathers, that the Lord has brought you out with a mighty hand and redeemed you.

> Know therefore that the Lord your God is God, the faithful God who keeps covenant and steadfast love with those who love him and keep his commandments.

> And because you hearken to these ordinances and keep and do them, the Lord your God will keep with you the covenant and the steadfast love

DEUTERONOMY 7:6-11

Realizing that it is possible to be tied to other humans or earth-bound entities as your Source of Power, and refusing to let that continue, means that you have to take responsibility for yourself. But that is a gift, a gift of power that no one can take away from you or control. For now the energy from that Power flows through you, from God, into your endeavors, or into the lives of other people.

chapter thirteen

The Only Moment
You Have Is This One

Happy is the man, or woman, who finds wisdom.

PROVERBS 3:13

My 1967 Datsun 1600 Sportster scooted along beneath me, full
of purring spiritedness, as my puppy, Molly, lay with her chin on
my knee, one eye opening now and then in response to my running
commentary. With the convertible top down, the sunny day
warmed my shoulders as it also touched the surrounding mountains
still capped with snow in May.

The thought came to me, "What if something were to happen
to me tonight, making this the last day of my life?"

I reflected on that and answered, aloud, "It would be all
right. It was a good day—not a spectacular day, but a good day.
What more can I ask than what I have at this very moment—a
beautiful sunny world, a neat little car, a loving puppy, joy."

"Joy!" I said. "But your world has fallen apart! You have lost the most important thing in your life, your marriage, which was your emotional and financial security!"

"That is true, but I . . ."

"How are you going to survive? Where will you get enough money to live on? What will you do about loneliness? Maybe when your book sells . . . . Or maybe you will meet a man . . ."

"I can't wait to be happy until those things happen because the only moment I have is this one. I have no guarantee that anything will happen beyond this very moment."

"Of course, but you know they *will* happen . . . !"

"Do I? What if this *were* my very last day, and I spent it planning to be happy when—and if—I make a lot of money or meet a new friend? *The only moment I have is this one!*"

"But how can you be happy when there are so many things that could go wrong, and probably will?"

I reflected on that a long time. Why was I joyful, energetic, full of life, in spite of a catastrophic loss and the very real possibility of severe problems in the days ahead?

I remembered James, in the New Testament, talking about this very thing when he said, "You do not know about tomorrow. What is your life? For you are a mist that appears for a little time and then vanishes. Instead you ought to say, 'If the Lord wills, we shall live and we shall do this or that.'"

Molly's loving glance confirmed my understanding. "I am happy because I like myself, right now, at this moment. That doesn't mean I don't want to change or that I don't have major goals for the future. I don't need to wait for another man to come into my life to love me; I don't need the assurance of lots of money; I don't need to wait until one of my books sells. Right now, at this moment, I know that God loves me, just as I am! Therefore, *I* like me, just as I am!"

This idea was confirmed by Mark, a friend who added another dimension to it. He said, "Perfect love casts out fear. Perfect love is the understanding that if you love yourself at this very moment, you don't have to dread the next moment, or the next year, or the next life. Nor are you afraid of the next person you are going to meet, wondering if he might do you in. Such love releases you to enjoy this moment, this person, free of anxiety.

"But," Mark went on, "the other discovery that added a new dimension to my life was that to lose my fright of what could happen allowed me to look at the people around me in a new light. I became aware of them, not as potential threats to my well-being, but as people also in the throes of problems and anxieties. Turning loose my qualms was like removing the thick window through which I had been viewing the other people in my world, able to see them but well-protected from them. Now I can ask them how they are, what is going on in their lives, without being defensive or anticipating that I will somehow be hurt. That faith frees me to be caring."

Joshua called his people to obedience, to the understanding that joy lay in following the covenant.

> *Choose this day whom you will serve;*
> *but as for me and my house, we will serve the Lord*
>
> JOSHUA 24:15

When God sent Joshua into the Promised Land, Joshua could have been afraid to move very far away from his Source of Power, but the Bible tells us that he took with him God's support.

> *Be strong and courageous, being careful to do according to all the law which Moses my servant commanded you; turn not from it to the right hand or to the left, that you may have good success wherever you go. This book of the law shall not depart out of your mouth, but you shall meditate on it day and night, that you may be careful to do according to all that is written in it...Be strong and of good courage; be not frightened, neither be dismayed; for the Lord your God is with you wherever you go*
>
> JOSHUA 1:1-9

On the television program *M*A*S*H*, Father Mulcahy said, "God put people on the earth so He could be here, too." If I discover the love of God through my inner self, then so do other people, and we can learn about God through each other. It may not look like the God we know, but it may present a new facet of God.

Our lives could be said to be like living on an island. God is the ocean, wide, endless, uncharted, but at the same time, as near as the water lapping the shore—familiar, present, and life-giving. If someone asks us to tell him about God, we would describe the part of the ocean we understand, but the person living on the other side of the island might describe God in very different terms.

Perhaps the ocean on my side of the island is almost always calm, but the other side of the island experiences high winds and high seas. Each of us has a very different view of God, but each is authentic; both of us will say that we "know what God is like," and we will both be right.

The Psalmist felt strongly about what God meant to him—no fly-by-night God, this one:

> Lord, thou has been our dwelling place
>   in all generations
> Before the mountains were brought forth,
>   or ever thou formed the earth and the world,
>   from everlasting to everlasting thou art God.
> For a thousand years in thy sight
>   are but as yesterday when it is past,
>   or as a watch in the night
>
> PSALM 90:1-4

Elaine, a woman who had every reason to be frightened of what life had in store for her, told me that she went through an experience of discovering that living this moment without fear of the next one was the only choice that made sense, because it was such a freeing experience.

In spite of facing terminal cancer, Elaine said, "Being fearful of what the next hour or the next experience holds gives away your power to that next hour so that you don't have it to use now, although it does give an excuse for not accepting responsibility. When the fears of anticipated pain were dispelled, I discovered a power I had never known. No longer was I using energy to protect myself from other people or to prepare myself for anticipated pain; I had strength left over to use on the important things in my life, now!

"To accept full responsibility for myself, to be responsible for my happiness right now, is power!" Elaine said. "It means that instead of waiting for someone else to look after me, I am in charge. That is power! Usable power! At first it's scary; then you get this heady feeling that comes from being in charge of your own life, you and God."

Ruth, a woman who lost her husband suddenly, found another positive effect of accepting responsibility and choosing to be happy right now, this moment. Trusting in God and no longer fearful of what lay ahead, she began to reach out to people around her. She discovered that each one made a contribution to her life. The last time I talked with her she had a large circle of friends and had decided that she would prefer many friends to one close and possibly limiting friendship.

Many religious people, Christians and non-Christians alike, think that the mandate of their faith is to tell someone else what to believe, as interpreted by the person who thinks he has the right message.

In the New Testament John tells the story of a woman who talked with Jesus and then went running off to tell others, saying,

Come and hear this man! He told me about myself!

JOHN 4:1-42

We all want to hear about ourselves, and we aren't really interested in hearing about someone else. We may listen politely, but chances are, it won't convince us of anything. When a person is freed from fear so that she can reach out to others, asking what is going on in their lives and sharing what is going on in hers, that opens the way to a new relationship. A non-defensive person who does not need to protect herself against other people's ideas is more likely to find people who are willing to talk and be open and honest.

A gift from God, this moment belongs to you and no one else. Because this is the only moment you may claim, don't wait for another. Lay hold of the power, the energy that belongs to this one. Use it! Enjoy it!

chapter fourteen

Soul Attacks

Of all the life accidents that happen to us, the most debilitating and most threatening to our faith are those involving close relationships—the loss of a friend, a marriage partner, or a family member because of death or a broken friendship. Even if we were never very close to God before, such an experience sends us scurrying to shake our fist at God, or at the very least, to ask, "Why me, God?"

The Twenty-second Psalm is a whole novel in itself, moving from despair to faith in graphic scenes. Beginning with "My God, my God, why hast thou forsaken me?" the words Jesus spoke from the cross centuries later, the stage is set for the story of despair, tragedy, and loss of faith.

> O my God, I cry by day, but you don't answer;
> and by night, but find no rest.

But, the Psalmist says, I do remember that my fathers trusted you, God, and you did deliver them. They trusted you, and you didn't let them down.

But he vacillates; the next scene shows our main character berating himself:

> But I am a worm, and no man;
>   scorned by men, and despised by the people.
> All who see me mock at me,
>   they make mouths at me, they wag their heads;
> He committed his cause to the Lord, let him deliver him;
>   let him rescue him, for he delights in him!

Yet the person does believe that God was not always absent from his life.

> Yet thou art he who took me from the womb;
>   thou did keep me safe upon my mother's breasts.

Nevertheless our hero feels deserted by the God who is supposed to be looking after him.

And he begins to tentatively ask God for help.

> Be not far from me,
> for trouble is near and there is none to help.

His lack of faith has dried up his energy source also:

> I am poured out like water,
>   and all my bones are out of joint;
> my heart is like wax,
>   it is melted within my breast;
> my strength is dried up like a potsherd
>   and my tongue cleaves to my jaws;
>   thou dost lay me in the dust of death.

Was there ever a better example of losing energy through lack of faith? Then he goes again into a recitation of his woes:

> Yea, dogs are round about me;
>   a company of evildoers encircle me;
>   they have pierced my hands and feet—
> I can count all my bones—
>   they stare and gloat over me;
> they divide my garments among them,
>   and for my raiment they cast lots.

And then it happens! God takes care of his problem, and our hero is overjoyed, singing the praises of God.

> Posterity shall serve him;
>   men shall tell of the Lord to the coming generation,
> and proclaim his deliverance to a people yet unborn,
>   that he has wrought it.

Thus he moved from anger and guilt to faith, hope, and joy.

Jesus too, on the cross, moved from anger at God, "My God, why have you forsaken me?" to acceptance and then faith, "Father, into your hands I commit my spirit!"

So much of loss is guilt for real or fancied failure on our part to do what we should have done. When we have lost someone, as in death, or are in danger of losing someone we love, as in divorce, guilt becomes an overriding emotion.

"If only I had worked harder, I wouldn't have lost my job... If only I had been a better mother... If only I had shown more love while she was alive..."

"If only" is the saddest and most futile phrase in the English language. The result is a loss of belief in yourself, a loss of faith in God.

Guilt serves no useful purpose; it only clouds our vision, making it impossible to see our situation clearly. The healthy person accepts responsibility but rejects guilt. But how? When our world is falling down around us, how do we have the understanding and the courage to deal with guilt?

First you have to recognize that guilt is what you are dealing with, for it will masquerade as anger or fear or pain.

On my first trip to New York in many years I was laying elaborate plans to enjoy the city. Getting away from home was a great idea; it would allow me to stand back and look at my situation, do some clear thinking about it.

The second night there, I made an important decision: to turn loose the relationship, to accept the fact that there was nothing more to be done. Feeling very relieved, I went to sleep. During the night I wakened with a headache. Strange, I thought, and managed to go back to sleep. The next morning the headache was so severe that I was sick to my stomach.

I asked myself, "Why do I have a headache when I made that positive decision last night? I should be feeling great, not sick." There was no question as to the cause; for me, a headache is always due to something negative in my life.

Two aspirin barely muted the misery, so I set out on my pre-planned activities for that day, hoping that ignoring the torment would make it go away. Each step on the cement sidewalks produced a throbbing pain as I dragged myself along, drained in spirit and unable to participate in the alive, exciting city around me.

Finally I told myself, "Are you going to let a headache ruin your visit to New York? Go to your desert and find out what is going on inside yourself to cause such agony."

Walking down Fifth Avenue, I came to St. Patrick's Cathedral and went in, the cool darkness soothing to my feverish brow. A lone meditator, I sat down and began to peel away the layers of distress, talking to myself as I did so.

"It was great that I figured out that I have to turn loose the relationship. But that was an intellectual decision, and my psyche is saying, 'No Way! I'm not going to turn loose a relationship that is as vital to my survival as this! I've got to keep trying to save it, otherwise I will feel so guilty!'

"Guilty? That implies that someone is assigning blame. Do you think that God . . .?"

I interrupted, "God is in as much pain as I am about

this ... it isn't a matter of who is to blame. He just wants me to remain faithful, and I'm trying to decide what that looks like at this moment."

"Then your choice is not whether to allow the divorce, but only what you are going to do with it."

"That is true, but my psyche is in mortal anguish. It is something like a heart attack in which part of the heart dies, causing great pain. Only this is my soul. When a vital relationship dies, part of the soul dies, causing pain. I am having a *soul attack!*"

I repeated that in an audible whisper, "That's what it is—a *soul attack*. I am grieving for the loss of a vital part of myself. The soul attacks will go on as that part of my soul dies, and I have to let it die. The soul attacks *will* continue, and that's all right! Painful, but all right, because I do not need to feel guilty about letting go; it is the healthy thing to do. God understands what is happening, and that's what matters. If I know that, I will come out of this a whole person."

Abruptly, my body relaxed, and I said, "Thank you," to an invisible Hearer.

I stood up, greatly relieved, satisfied that I had indeed found the cause of my pain. As I walked out the door of the cathedral, the excruciating, incapacitating headache evaporated, leaving my mind clear and free. Suddenly I wanted to dance, to shout, to tell the world I had been healed! Anyone seeing me might have thought I was possessed.

Now I know what miracles are made of.

Jesus said to him, "Rise, take up your pallet, and walk." And at once the man was healed, and he took up his pallet and walked.

JOHN 5:9

How do you recognize a soul attack when it is happening? It may be accompanied by tears, but not necessarily. Now, months after the event that caused the soul attacks, when I begin to talk about the death of the marriage, my voice becomes hoarse; I get a full feeling in my sinuses and around my eyes; my body may begin to tense. Crying is a total body experience, not just water coming out of the tear ducts.

Several times since that experience in New York I have wondered what would have happened if I had attributed the headache to some physical ailment and gone immediately to a medical doctor. He would have given me medication, probably strong drugs, considering the severity of the condition. Since the cause was not physical, if I had not attempted to find the real cause, chances are the headache would have gone on for days, completely ruining my trip to New York and preventing some of the good things that came out of it, such as the idea for this book.

Very few people will ever realize that their pain is a soul attack. There are several reasons for that.

One, if something hurts, people usually take aspirin or a stronger medication. They don't put up with pain; no one has to these days.

Two, all pains are presumed to have physical causes, with little thought given to the possibility of psychic origins. In spite of the fact that I understood my body well enough to know that the headache was undoubtedly of psychic origin, my first reaction was to tell myself to go back to sleep, that it was probably just the excitement of being in New York and would be gone in the morning.

How many of these reasons for a headache have you heard recently?

† crooked position while sleeping
† an allergy
† cigarette smoke
† air conditioning
† sudden cold weather/sudden hot weather
† something eaten

Three, few people take time to honestly ask the tough questions about what is *really* going on inside themselves.

Four, if we feel guilty, we think we deserve suffering. Somehow, hurting assuages our guilt, but only for a little while; then we are ready for it to go away.

Americans go to great lengths to avoid pain or to get rid of it. For some people, spending money is one of the ways to get their mind off their troubles. A woman buying a dress or a hot fudge sundae or a man buying a new boat or a steak dinner, both having soul attacks because of a major loss in their lives, are seeking ways to camouflage hurt.

Others find different ways, some destructive. Buying beyond their means, finding another sexual relationship, drinking—all can be ways to escape pain.

> *Therefore I tell you, do not be anxious about your life, what you shall eat or what you shall drink, nor about your body, what you shall put on. Is not life more than food, and the body more than clothing? Look at the birds of the air; they neither sow nor reap nor gather into barns, and yet your heavenly Father feeds them. Are you not of more value than they? And which of you by being anxious can add one cubit to his span of life?*
>
> *And why are you anxious about clothing? Consider the lilies of the field, how they grow; they neither toil nor spin, yet I tell you, even Solomon in all his glory was not arrayed like one of these.*
>
> *Therefore do not be anxious . . . but seek first his kingdom and his righteousness, and all these things shall be yours as well.*
>
> MATTHEW 6:25-33

The manuscript for this book had been written; I was in the process of doing the final re-reading before it would go to the publisher and had worked late the night before.

"Do not be anxious about your body . . ."

Never had those words been so clearly etched on my brain as I lay in bed that spring morning, the dawning light not yet seeping in behind the drapes on the window. I had slept, fitfully, waking several times in tears. My puppy could never stand to have me cry and each time came to lick my face. Such caring comfort!

The night before, as I was preparing for sleep, I had found a small lump in one breast during a routine self-examination. My tears came not from fear of dying of cancer, although the danger was not to be minimized. Rather, I had to deal with two fears that had long been part of myself. The fear of what breast cancer would mean to me as a woman, and the fear of going through such an illness alone.

I had to deal with my anguish relating to marriage vows, "in sickness and in health, as long as we both shall live." I feared going through the Darkness without the person who had promised to be there through the pain and even to the death.

One of the Psalms talks about this:

> It is not an enemy who taunts me—
>   then I could bear it;
> It is not an adversary who deals insolently with me—
>   then I could hide from him.
> But it is you, my equal,
>   my companion, my familiar friend.
> We used to hold sweet converse together;
>   within God's house we walked in fellowship.

There was, of course, the question of the cancer itself. I *would* die someday, from some dreadful malady or other, but one of the lessons I learned was that I was not afraid to die, and, more important, that I was not afraid to live.

At least, I thought I wasn't, but the prospect of having my body mutilated by breast surgery made me pause to consider what life would be like. I like being a woman; I would like another relationship sometime. Would this make that impossible and destroy part of who I am?

So the first decision I made was to not go to the doctor immediately; I made an appointment for five days later. I knew there was a possibility that as soon as the lump was verified, doctors would be palpating, punching, and cutting my body. So I took those five days to "celebrate" my body, "perfect" and beautiful as it is, for it is that, not necessarily in physical terms but in terms of God's creation. For five days, I enjoyed living inside my body, using it in happy ways, running, jumping rope, climbing a tree, feeling the freedom of a whole, healthy body.

But over and over I found myself looking backward, thinking "if only..." So I made a poster to put on the refrigerator that said, "You can't see ahead if you keep looking backward."

I reread this manuscript's passage about the lilies of the field and found my answer to my first fear. Jesus said, "Is not life more than food and the body more than clothing?" And I added, Is not personhood more than the body? In being afraid that somehow I would be fundamentally different if I had breast surgery, I was allowing myself to be defined by my body, not by my soul.

"Do not be anxious about your life... nor about your body, but seek first his kingdom." That was my answer! If I could not be quite the same person physically, then I would become a different person, a new person with new restrictions and new possibilities and new ways of seeking the Kingdom!

Whether or not the lump turned out to be malignant would be irrelevant, for I had wrestled with my angel again and met God face to face.

The other fear, of going through the Valley of the Shadow by myself, was more difficult. As it was close to Easter, I was reading the Easter story and came to the place in that terrible scene where Jesus was in agony, praying about his impending death, and came back over and over to find his friends asleep. When the ones he thought he could depend on were not there, Jesus did not use that as an excuse to avoid keeping his covenant with God and going through with the death scene. Jesus' decision was to confirm that God was still faithful and to be trusted. "Not my will, but thine, be done."

That realization became a reaffirmation that God will be there with me in the Darkness; but God is also to be found in my caring children and friends. I am not alone!

"Today is the celebration of the victory of our God.
Thanks be to God!"

"Seeking first the Kingdom" means accepting the losses that are inevitable in this life, grieving over them, acknowledging our share of responsibility, recognizing the soul attacks when they come, and moving on to whatever God has in store for us.

That is faith and that is power!

chapter fifteen

Wrestling With Your Angel

Since a sustaining faith does not spring full-grown when we are baptized or dedicated, every life experience has the potential of enriching that faith and rejuvenating the body. An understanding of the Spirit that lives within us can provide a source of energy that can give new zeal and enjoyment to our every day.

One type of encounter that can be especially significant is coming face to face with your angel.

Many people believe that angels are to be found only in the Bible. Not so!

Let's look at Genesis for one of the most memorable instances of a visit from an angel.

Jacob knew many angels; over and over the Bible tells about visits to Jacob from angels or the presence of angels. One incident was the famous story of the angels climbing and descending the ladder (from which the song "Jacob's Ladder" originated). As memorable and famous is Jacob's wrestling match with an angel.

Jacob was scared, really scared. As a young man he had cheated his brother, Esau, out of his birthright by trading him a bowl of soup for it. Then, fearing the consequences of his actions, he ran away to another country where he lived for twenty years, married two wives, and had eleven sons. (Daughters weren't counted.) Now he was returning to his home, eager to see his mother and the hills of home, but knowing he must at last face his brother.

He had run away because he was afraid Esau would kill him; now he was again afraid for his life. When word came to him that Esau was coming to meet him with four hundred men, Jacob panicked. He split his party into two groups so that if one was destroyed, the other would be left. Picking out the best of his cattle, he prepared wave after wave of servants bearing gifts of goats, sheep, cows, and camels for his brother, Esau. Sending his family on to a safe place, Jacob was left alone.

Now it was evening, the night before he would encounter his brother, and Jacob was terrified. He lay down to sleep, and, as so often happens in times of great stress, he didn't sleep very well; he had a troubled dream in which he spent all night wrestling with a man, an angel from God.

Can we imagine what that must have been like? It was not romping, as children might tussle, or a make-believe vision; it was anything but a calm event, as the two men rolled and struggled together. Panting, grunting, writhing, they strove for hours in that highly emotion-charged night, the Bible says, "until the breaking of the day."

But when it was over, Jacob was amazed that he was still alive instead of having been destroyed by the angel of God. Jacob gave thanks that he was still alive after such an experience. Jacob called the name of the place Peniel, "for I have seen God face to face, and my life is preserved."

Jacob was a rascal and a coward. He had cheated his brother out of a birthright; deceived his old, blind father; used questionable practices to insure getting the choice livestock from his uncle; fled rather than tell his uncle that he was running off with his uncle's daughters and grandchildren. But it is one of the stories in the Old Testament that gives us hope that, even in our iniquitous condition, God may love us anyway. If he could do it for Jacob, there is hope for us.

But there was a lot of guilt in Jacob's inner soul that night, and it was that guilt that made him willing to come close to God. He needed relief, after all those years of living with his crimes. He had reached the point when he could no longer put off the moment of truth.

Sometimes, when that happens, we turn and face the fear, and, with God's help, conquer it. Jacob had enough understanding of what was happening that he refused to let the angel go until the angel took away his guilt. "He said, 'I will not let you go, unless you bless me.'"

As happens a number of times in the Bible when a person's name is changed to indicate a significant alteration in that person's character, the angel gave Jacob a new name, Israel, because he had power with men and with God.

Then, just at dawn, when Jacob won out over the angel, the messenger of God touched Jacob in a final gesture, leaving a permanent scar on his thigh.

Jacob is an excellent example of our own fears. Far from being a perfect human, Jacob had done some very bad things. Just as important as his trepidations about the other people in his life was Jacob's fear of God, that Being who had been with him through it all and to whom he felt responsible. Over and over God had told Jacob that he was loved by God, and yet, in this story, Jacob is again scared to face God because of what he had done. Guilt produces terrible anxieties.

But once again, God sent an angel to tell Jacob that in spite of Jacob's bad habits, God still loves him and will continue to be with him.

In the morning, when Jacob wakened, he realized that he had spent the night in the company of God. He said, "I have seen God face to face."

Where had he seen God? Within his own being, inside himself, in his dreams. He had wrestled with the God within him—and won.

Then, the next day, because he had met God that night, he

had the marvelous experience of encountering God again. When he and Esau neared each other, Esau came running and hugged and kissed Jacob, and they both cried. As Jacob realized he had been forgiven by his brother and by God, he said to Esau, "I have seen your face, as though I had seen the face of God." To see forgiveness in Esau's face was to accept the forgiveness of God, as though God were present. To see love in another person's face is to see God at that moment in that place.

Just think what an incredible day that was for Jacob! In the same day, his relationships with God and with his brother had been repaired. After twenty years of guilt, it was a day to rejoice, to give thanks, to dance, to celebrate!

Can you imagine him greeting people, his face alive, animated; shaking hands, moving quickly among the company, his body's zeal rejuvenated? Even the painful thigh was probably forgotten in the joy of this incredible day! Forgiveness can bring healing of mind and body!

If Jacob had not met God face to face the night before and wrestled with Him, he would not have recognized God in his brother's face the next day.

Only if we care enough about what God thinks of us and have the courage to go close to God and talk about it can the important questions of our lives be answered.

The story of the Prodigal Son in Luke (15) describes a threatening father who turned out to be a forgiving father, and a loving one, because the son dared return and ask forgiveness. "It was fitting to make merry and be glad, for this your brother was dead, and is alive; he was lost, and is found."

Of course, we are frightened by God, but if we are not terrified of God, we treat Him as being unimportant; we ignore Him; He has no power to change us—or to *save* us!

When we are not afraid of God and do not go into His presence trembling, we live our lives as if *we* were in charge—until a life accident teaches us a lesson. Suddenly we start looking for answers. Where can we find them? From someone else? No one but the God within us knows us well enough to call us to account, to help find the answers, but most important, to forgive us.

"Only a God who can terrify can save us!"[13]

But there is a part of the story that is rarely noticed. Jacob was left with a permanent disfigurement from the encounter with God. When we come close to the God within us as imperfect, inadequate, frightened people, having to admit our failures, our greed, our unfaith, we cannot wrestle with God and win, without carrying the scars forever. Remember, it is the God within us that we are wrestling with. Cutting out greed, mistrust, unfaith, has to leave scars where they were. But scars can be beautiful if they serve to remind us of God's love.

I know how Jacob felt.

The spring day was beautiful. I had just had a pleasant lunch with a friend and was walking to my car when my attorney drove into the parking lot. He greeted me and said, "I have to give you some bad news; you lost the case we appealed to the state Supreme Court."

We went on talking about it briefly, and I left.

Driving down the highway in my car, I suddenly began raging, talking louder and louder until I was shouting.

In the midst of my screaming, the question came, "Why are you raging? This is out of proportion to the news you just received. Why?"

"It means the loss of a lot of money!"

"You know that money is only money; it is not soul-destroying in itself. So you lose $3,000; that's a lot of money, but it isn't the end of the world."

"But this added problem could mean that I will come out much worse financially in the divorce settlement, and I will be blamed since I had the accident!"

"Even that is not enough to bring on this kind of response. What is the real problem? What are you afraid of?"

One after the other I listed my fears, reciting them in a loud voice; the list was long. My hands were shaking; my legs were wobbly as I continued driving down the highway.

"But," the voice said to me, "none of those is bad enough to be the 'enemy.' Reach deeper; of what are you most afraid? Who is the enemy?"

There was silence as I moved deeper within myself and searched for the answer. Then I said, "The enemy isn't my husband; the enemy isn't the loss of money; the enemy isn't . . ."

Then I saw the answer. "My enemy is my own fear. I'm afraid I don't have what it takes to make it. I'm afraid God will not love me because I don't deserve to be loved. I'm afraid I can't make it alone and God won't think I'm good enough to help me!"

"Look at yourself," the voice said. "You are a frightened, inhibited, groveling person, allowing money and other people to tie you in knots. You are trembling, your strength is being dissipated in fear and anger. Is that who you want to be?

"No!" I shouted. "No one can do anything to me unless I allow it. Nothing—lack of money, loss of love, or fear—is going to deter me from being the person I want to be!"

"And who is that?"

"A woman who is faithful to her covenant with God."

Then into my mind came a Bible verse I didn't realize I knew.

"Yea, though they kill me, yet will I not forsake Thee."

The presence of the angel who had challenged me was as real as the steering wheel in my hands. In anger and desperation I had wrestled with her, trying to justify my fear, my failures, my lack of faith, to blame them on someone else.

I could not forsake the covenant to be faithful I had made with God long ago and renewed over and over through the years. Now I understood that that meant being faithful even in the midst of loss of love, money, or anything or everything else in my life.

When all was gone, I still had the assurance of God's love, and at that moment I reclaimed that. God had thought me worthy of his most intimate concern in the person of the angel! Thanks be to God!

To my surprise I had a sudden and immediate reaction to the experience. Where I had been weak, exhausted, shaking, I felt a surge of energy coming from outside myself and flowing through me. Instead of going home and collapsing, as had been my first thought, I discovered the potential energy from my soul being turned into kinetic energy, and my brain went into high gear. At that moment I could have challenged the world with my pen! Back home at my typewriter, I wrote down my encounter with my angel.

It is not natural for humans to face fear directly; we are masters at avoiding it. Indeed, most people would rather not face themselves at such a profound level. What happens if we refuse to be accosted by the angel from God?

Actually, it is easy to avoid that confrontation by saying:

† you don't believe in angels
† you have no right to challenge God
† God will take care of things without your doing anything so drastic

One effective way to handle fear is to encounter it in our dreams. Jacob was not ready to face Esau, so his inner self, in a dream, helped him cope with the panic that was rising up out of him. Esau was not even present; the terror, the *shetan*, was coming from inside Jacob and that was where it had to be confronted. Facing fear, however it is done, whether in an inner vision in the broad daylight of our everyday lives, or in the equally frightening depth of our dreams, will strip the fright of its power over us.

Jesus' words and life showed us that we can expect terrors; we can anticipate trouble; we can plan on apprehension. God does not cause or prevent the wars that humankind has brought about, but when we stand in the bomb crater, dreading the discovery of our child's body in the rubble, God is standing there with us, weeping also. God does not promise to remove the evils, but only to help us dispel our fear of them.

When Jacob finally met Esau face to face after twenty years of living in fear because of what he had done to his brother, the fear was dispelled by his brother's forgiveness, and Jacob could recognize that God was present at that moment, for " . . . to see your face is to see the face of God."

However, it is impossible to go through such a soul-wrenching experience without leaving permanent scars. In the Genesis story Jacob set out at daybreak to join his wives and children, but shortly after the sun rose he had to stop because his thigh, where the angel had touched him, was so painful. If you dare come close enough to God to tell Him your anger and to listen to His response, you have good reason to be terrified, for such a powerful Being could destroy you. That experience cannot help but leave you with a memory that will never go away, a mark on your soul, if not on your body, for you will never be the same again.

That experience left an excision mark where the angel had touched me, where the panic, the unfaith, had been cut out of my soul. It did not heal and become merely a scar immediately. Over and over I wanted to use fear as an excuse. If you let other people know you are afraid, they will feel sorry for you, do things to protect you, or give you gifts to make you feel better. But the memory of the visit from the angel gave me courage to demand faith from myself instead of fear.

Even though you may be a new person because of your experience with your angel, maybe even, like Jacob, a person with a new name, you will bear scars where the angel touched you, for you cannot alter so basic a part of yourself without leaving a scar.

Then, too, an unexpected result of the renewal of your faith covenant may be a surge of energy that will send you into rewarding endeavors.

The important thing is not what happens to you; it's what you do with it that counts. To be true to yourself is to honor your faith covenant with God. To confront yourself at the deepest level is to wrestle with God.

chapter sixteen

Sharing the Holy Spaces

There is nothing that requires more energy or faith than human relationships. Nor is there any other facet so full of potential joy and fulfillment. To our dismay, those very intimacies may cause the most profound pain.

The poetry of "The Prophet" expresses this idea:

For even as love crowns you so shall he crucify you.
Even as he is for your growth so is he for your pruning.
Even as he ascends to your height and caresses your tenderest branches
*   that quiver in the sun,*
So shall he descend to your roots and shake them in their clinging to
*   the earth.*
Like sheaves of corn he gathers you unto himself.
He threshes you to make you naked.
He sifts you to free you from your husks.
He grinds you to whiteness.
He kneads you until you are pliant.

And then he assigns you to his sacred fire,
that you may become sacred bread for God's sacred feast.
All these things shall love do unto you that you may know the secrets
of your heart and in that knowledge become a fragment of
life's heart.

We hear a different theme in most marriage ceremonies today.

I take thee . . . to have and to hold . . .
For richer or poorer; in sickness and in health . . .
From this day forth and forever more . . .
So long as we both shall live . . .

And so from this day and forever, we belong to each other. But what is it that belongs to each other?

"I once watched, appalled, as a young couple in their marriage ceremony used their individual tapers to light a single candle, and then blew out their own candles, as the minister said, "And the two shall become one!" How poignantly descriptive of a relationship headed down the wrong road.

What is it that is no longer separate, but one? Their money, their abilities, their bodies, their relatives, their faith? Any or all of these.

Women clearly understand this to mean that they shall subordinate their own beings to that of their husbands. No longer separate; they belong together in mystical, romantic union—*one!* Men have no such understanding, for society does not require such a commitment of personhood on their part.

Only a fraction of the couples participating in a marriage ceremony have adequate discussion of the rite, and when, after many years the man still shows no such commitment to one-ness, the woman wonders what went wrong, feeling that surely she must have failed somewhere.

The fault lies not in their diverse commitments to the relationship, but rather in a failure to understand the nature of faith. Faith is not a shared experience; it is a covenant between each individual and God. How, then, does one develop and nourish

126

faith and be true to a marriage or friendship commitment? How does one give the necessary devotion to a friend or mate and still retain the freedom to become the person God would have us be?

If we are to be free within the bonds of marriage; if we are to hold each other with an open hand in friendship, what would the relationship look like?

It would be a "sharing of the Holy Spaces."[14]

First, each one within the relationship must decide what is sacred within himself or herself. Then they come together, not to give away that part of themselves, nor to exchange it, but to share it. That part must remain sacred, not open to alteration by the other person, modified only by desire and permission of the individual. But it is that part which is most fundamentally ourselves which is also the most precious. To share any less than that would be to trivialize the relationship.

Sharing the Holy Spaces in marriage is no different than in other close relationships.

So often we refuse to be truly open, to admit what is really bothering us at a particular moment. Describing joy or pleasure is not difficult, but admitting pain or fear makes us seem less than in control. And society demands that we must *never* appear not to be in control!

Out of the don't-show-your-emotions generations born in earlier years of this century has come a group of people, particularly men, that believes showing emotion is a sign of weakness.

Recently I watched a close friend go through a terrible life accident. Observing his face during a conversation with him, I saw that even when he was saying serious, painful things, no emotion was showing on his face. And yet, there had to be incredible agony going on deep in the sacred part of him. But he would not share it with anyone. The tension was showing itself in other ways, such as sudden explosive anger when dealing with strangers. It was with those close to him that he could not describe his true feelings.

Again, as in the chapter on healing ourselves, one is reminded of the statement, "If they did not cry, rage, call for help, or remember painful events, their bodies seemed to do those things for them." My friend's blood pressure was very high, and he ate antacids like candy. He apparently did not know that sharing one's pain, which is sacred to each of us, is to give the other person a gift. In return for that gift of pain, a gift of caring is offered. No antacid or blood pressure medicine in the world can compare with a hug and the words, "It's all right; I'm here; don't be afraid." I did not feel I could intrude into my friend's Holy Spaces without his permission, so I could not say the caring words.

When, over and over in our day-to-day intimate relationships, the response from a person is silence, the normal reaction is to wonder what we have done to cause such a negative response. Perhaps we back off or alter our method of approach, which is exactly what is expected. We learn to program each other to do what we want done, and silence is one of the ways to do that. Silence is a powerful tool, or weapon, depending on how it is used.

The opposite of love is not hate; it is indifference. The most devastating thing we can do to someone is to ignore them. All of us know children who do naughty, unacceptable things knowing they will be punished, but it is their only way of getting attention from parents who ignore them. Even punishment is preferable to unconcern.

We make the mistake of assuming that silence must surely be better than angry shouting, but in reality, you can get hold of a person's anger; it is out front, available. A person's silence is untouchable, an insidious form of intimidation, for it leaves the object of the silence feeling unworthy and unimportant.

A person chooses as a friend someone who is like himself or herself, but is less likely to marry that person. For a marriage partner, most people want someone who has traits unlike theirs, to fill in their gaps. At first, the traits are admired and envied, but soon after the marriage begins, it is not uncommon for one mate to begin to tear down the other, precisely because he or she feels envious of those very traits, and inferior to the mate.

Knowing our own strengths, having faith in ourselves and the God within us, allows us to accept the other person without judgment.

A survey was taken of why people married, and then the same people were asked why they divorced. Over and over, the reasons were the same. That which was felt to be a strength at the time of the marriage had become a negative; the sacred qualities were no longer accepted.

For example, a woman admired the way a man handled money, guarding it carefully, being a good money manager and provider. In later years, his conservatism with money became unbearable as he developed into a penny pincher, insisting on putting money into a savings account instead of taking a chance on more lucrative uses of the money.

A man was attracted to a woman by her vivaciousness, her ability to never be at loss for words, when he felt inadequate at that point. In later years, her talkativeness became a point of irritation and he began to refuse to go out with her, but he was unwilling to tell her the real reason.

A woman whose father had been erratic in his decision-making was pleased to find a mate who was deliberate and dependable, but his deliberateness turned out to be procrastination. By the time she realized that her "dependable" husband was really afraid to make a decision, she had become a nagging wife. A counselor helped her to see that her husband had married her precisely because she was the kind of a woman who could make decisions. That left her with two choices: to try to get her husband to change, or to continue the pattern of making the decisions. She chose the latter, but a few years later her husband asked for a divorce, saying that he felt "powerless," not "in charge."

There must be freedom within the marriage for changes over the years, as our understanding of our Holy Spaces deepens or alters. How much energy is expended in being irritated by small idiosyncrasies: She never remembers to put gas in the car; he always parks so that the driveway is blocked.

A very intelligent man decided to marry a certain woman because she was more intelligent than the other woman he was considering. As the years went on, he took less time to keep up with his reading, although he was a professional man, while his wife spent more time, increasing her vocabulary and knowledge of national and world affairs. He was irritated by her knowledge, but his irritation was actually his own fear of being inadequate. His answer to that situation was to return to the first woman he had rejected years before because he felt more comfortable, less threatened.

If that man had accepted his own "sacredness," his unique and valuable abilities, he would not have been jealous of his wife.

A young woman was "wild" as a teenager and married a man who was "solid," by her terminology. He demanded that she settle down, which she did. Some years later she was considering divorce because he was too "straight-laced." "Solid" or "straight-laced" are the same things, depending on your vantage point.

In a play which I co-authored, a couple, John and Amanda, were traveling through time, stopping at churches at various intervals in the twentieth century, hoping to find the Children of the Promise, as described in Micah 4, which said that those who walk in the Lord's path will sit under their own fig tree, free from fear.

Three times Amanda and John came to Earth, searching for the Children of the Promise. Each time John declared that the Children were not in that place, for they were doing terrible things to each other. But Amanda thought she found them in each place, for she shared a part of herself, and the people returned that gift, while John held himself aloof, sitting in judgment. Each time, Amanda departed reluctantly with John, but each time she begged that the people in this spot be given another chance to become the Children of the Promise.

Finally, on a day in the present year, they return yet again to the same small town in Idaho. It has taken Amanda many years to come to believe in herself enough to have the courage to question her husband, and she suggests that perhaps he is looking in the wrong place for the Children. She tells him that unless the Promise is within us, we will never see it in anyone else.

John comes to understand that idea through his relationship with Amanda, rather than being threatened by it, and they decide to stay there to become part of the Children of the Promise.

The crucial message of the play is that until we work out the relationships with those closest to us, in other words, share the Holy Spaces, we cannot adequately deal with those "out there." Our dreams, however high-flown and desirable, can be realized only after we learn to accept ourselves and those intimate with us.

When our Holy Spaces are accepted by "significant others" in our lives, it frees us from the fear of rejection. Fear is an insidious thief, sneaking in to steal the energy we need for our jobs or our relationships. When the fear is removed, the resulting power is ours to use. That is what "empowering" means; freeing up our energy to be employed as we see fit.

In the chapter on *shetans*, we learned that it is up to us to control the *shetan* that rises out of our need to be persons of worth. It is possible to do that by ourselves, but it is much easier when someone close to us affirms our Holy Spaces.

Unless we recognize that there is a sacred part of us, we can never see the sacred part in another person, and we certainly can't share that understanding with another. That sacred part is the image of God that we all seek to emulate.

Jesus said, "The Kingdom of God is within you." Surely that is what we are talking about here.

When a person appears to be "strong," it may be assumed that he has the ability to protect himself better than other people, to create a thicker wall. But in actuality, to be strong may be to believe in yourself, in that sacred part, to "know in whom I have believed," to know the God within.

I quote from my own Journal, written at a time of questioning what strength really looked like. "Being strong allows you to know at the same time you don't know. It allows you to say with conviction what you know and at the same time to say to the other person, 'Tell me what you believe so that I may learn about faith from you.'"

That is sharing the Holy Spaces.

There are rare times when we need to enclose ourselves in a cage, only sticking out our hand to shake hands if necessary, to allow time for the psyche to heal. It's not unlike the body's need to be put into isolation for healing.

We might prevent some of those times if we allowed ourselves to share the Holy Spaces with others. Many times we decline to be truly present with each other, refusing to reveal anything of value from within ourselves, either out of fear of being hurt in our vulnerability, or of feeling that what we have to offer is not good enough.

In the famous passage on marriage in Ephesians 5, Paul understands the very important concept that only if a man loves himself first can he love his wife. But it must be equally true for the woman to love herself if she is to love her husband. In other words, she must know what is sacred within her if she is to love and respect anyone else, especially her husband.

A few marriage ceremonies are beginning to reflect the New Age, the global awareness. Contemporary marriage covenants are seen in terms of creatively contributing to the total human adventure of civilization, toward the well-being of all humankind.

Some young couples have a sensitivity that their marriage is not alone, but part of every family on earth and of the whole human family. It is a reflection of the new awareness of the oneness of God's creation.

In the traditional marriage, still very much present today, the man's commitment is to support the wife and family, while the wife's is to "love and honor." "Obey" is seldom heard now, but her commitment is still total, while his may end with the finances.

Being truly present takes on different forms. A woman translates her commitment into nurturing, with her love offering for her family being food. Basic to women's roles (at least, until the generation now choosing mates) is the fact that the way to show love to the family is to provide food as it is needed, but more than that, food that is nutritious, appetizing, and healthful.

For the man, his love offering is the paycheck he brings home. Because the world measures worth in dollars and cents, his offering seems to be the more important, and since the woman accepts that criterion, she may feel that her gift is inferior. She strives her whole life to fight the impossible battle, to make her gift as valuable, as sacred, as that of the man. If food is all that she has to offer, then when that is no longer needed (after the children have left the nest), her feelings that her gifts are no longer needed may become intense, and she may try to prove her worth in terms of dollars and cents by getting a job.

When women come to believe that what they bring to the marriage is as valid as the man's, then they can truly come together to share equally the Holy Spaces.

As a result of this situation in American life, the man carries what is often an unbearably heavy burden. Since his offering of money to his family is so important in the eyes of the world, he must make that offering the very best possible to prove that he is doing right by his family. He may remain in an unsatisfying job or feel trapped by having to provide more and more, resulting in high blood pressure and other stress-related conditions.

The sexual component is a crucial part of what is sacred within a relationship. Making love is a gift two people give each other, a gift not to be given or taken lightly, but with joy.

It is said that bad sex can destroy a marriage, but good sex does not necessarily make a good marriage. The difference is not the act itself, but whether or not in that event the sacred part of ourselves is offered, not to manipulate, but for sharing, and then whether or not it is accepted by the other person, not for usurpation or using for our own ends, but for coming to understand ourselves in relation to that other person. In making love, each is completely vulnerable to the other, and it provides what could be opportunity for the most profound sharing of the Holy Spaces that is available to humans.

In the chapter on Pain we looked at Job's relationship with the God within him. Our relationships with the significant other people in our lives has many of the same qualities as the one we have with our God. In fact, they are likely to look very much the same. Remember when Jacob saw God in his brother's face?

You will discover when you share your pain and receive a gift in return that the relationship moves to a higher level, for it was not just a cursory exchange on the time of day or the weather.

Job raged at God, daring to bare his soul to the one Being who could destroy it. But only a God who can terrify can save. And Job's willingness, in his desperation, to go close enough to rage at God allowed the relationship to move to a higher level, where God could pour out blessings, which would have been impossible at the lower level.

Relationships are not unlike that, either in a marriage or in a friendship.

Ruth and Naomi had such a friendship, for with profound emotion, Ruth said to Naomi, "Don't ask me to leave you, for where you go I will go, and where you lodge I will lodge; your people shall be my people, and your God my God; where you die I will die, and there will I be buried. May the Lord do so to me and more also if even death parts me from you" (Ruth 1:15-18). This was a commitment of love!

Helen and Margaret had been friends for years, sharing most of the events that happen in the lives of young families, but, more than that, talking about their dreams and their hopes. Each of them would have called their relationship a close one.

One day Margaret inadvertently became part of what appeared to be a conspiracy to oust Helen from an important position in an organization to which they both belonged. In actuality it happened without Margaret's consent, but she was unable to do anything about it. Their friendship was in jeopardy.

If it had not been a vital friendship to both of them, it would have been allowed to dwindle away, one feeling hurt, the other saying it was too bad, but there was nothing she could do about it. But theirs was a significant friendship.

However, each of them was afraid to encounter the other. (How often *fear* incapacitates us!)

Margaret said to herself, "Helen will refuse to speak to me, or order me out of her sight."

Helen said, "Margaret will be defensive and refuse to talk to me."

Finally, it was Helen who got up the courage to go to Margaret, in spite of the fact it would appear that she was the victim. (Remember Job!)

Helen's anger was great, and the scene was a stormy one as they laid out their pain and their fears. It could be said that they raged at each other.

Suddenly Margaret stopped the conversation and said, "Helen, why did you come to talk to me?"

Helen stopped, pondering that. "Because I had to know if you had done what you did because you were angry with me for some reason," she said finally.

"But," Margaret said, "if I was that angry, you could have just written me off as a disgruntled friend who tried to do you in. Why did you come?"

Helen knew the answer to that. "Because I cared so much about our friendship that I had to do something about it!"

Margaret put her arms around Helen and said, "You cared enough to risk being honest with me. Thank you for that gift!"

When they parted, it was with a new relationship between them, much deeper and more solid. Chances are, it would never reach that crisis point again, but if it did, either of them could go to the other and be free to "rage" until it had been resolved.

Many times the criticism coming from a mate or a friend is not intended to tear down, but rather is the result of caring enough about the relationship to challenge it, to call it to responsibility.

Marriage and friendships are by far the largest users of our energy—especially our psychic energy. An emotional confrontation usually leaves us feeling as if we had done a day of physical work. For that reason, everyone needs a place to retreat, a place where no effort is required, to rechange our Source of

Power. Within a marriage this is more difficult, but crucial nevertheless.

The dynamics of a growing relationship, either in marriage or friendship, are not unlike those of our relationship with God. Sharing the Holy Spaces requires first that we know what is sacred within us, and then that we be willing to share that with our friends or mate and to accept that which is sacred to them.

Because more psychic energy is used in relationships, the more we learn about "sharing the Holy Spaces," the less energy will be wasted and the more we will have to use toward new and more fulfilling friendships.

chapter seventeen

Self-Care Is Not Selfish

God does not love all the people in the world; He loves every single person, one by one. More specifically, he loves you! and me!

In John 3:16, when God loves the whole world, we must remember that "whosoever" means you and me!

> To all who received him, who believed in his name, he gave power
> to become children of God; who were born, not of blood nor of the
> will of the flesh nor of the will of man, but of God
>
> JOHN 1:12-13

Another assurance that God cares about every single person is the 14th verse of John 10, "I am the good shepherd; I know my own and my own know me."

One of the Lessons in faith I learned was one I had had to un-learn.

For a long time there has been a misconception making the rounds, disguised as Truth. It looks like this:

† Jesus First
† Others Second
† Yourself Last

The first three letters of each line make up the word "JOY." I can still see that sign hanging on the wall of my Sunday School class in a country church in Iowa. For most of fifty years I believed that, developing a guilt complex equal to all the other guilt complexes inherent in that philosophy.

I remember clearly how as a child at summer church camp we were brought together for "Morning Watch." A leader would read a scripture, then we would scatter, each to a separate place, alone, to meditate and pray.

Those were some of the longest ten minutes of my life, for I looked around surreptitiously at all the other campers who were praying. Everyone knew Jesus but me!

Only recently have I come to understand just how destructive that idea was.

I could never put the motto into practice, but I didn't know why. Instead, I merely accepted the guilt and felt inferior to all those other people out there who, I believed, were able to accomplish what I could not, put everyone else first, especially "Jesus."

Out of that grew a huge array of martyrs, especially among mothers, who gave up everything, including their identity as persons, as they subverted their own wishes and needs to those of their children and husbands. I even remember reading a quip that said, "Martyr, thy name is Mother."

What I have only recently come to understand is that if you don't love yourself *first*, you can never love anyone, either the "others" or Jesus.

Self-love, far from being a Sin, as we were taught as children, *must* happen first. Self-care means looking after yourself. That is *not* selfish, for to be a whole person you must have friends, and therefore you will do what it takes to have friends, that is, nurture your friendships. To consider only your own desires leaves you very lonely, and that is not taking care of yourself.

When a person goes for counseling, the counselor will likely talk about the three aspects of our lives; self-care, relationships, vocation. All three are important and need to be balanced in our lives, but we often throw ourselves out of balance by failing to nurture one of the areas adequately.

When you think of men who are past the age of forty, how many friends are they likely to have? Many of them have not one male friend; their only friend is their wife. That helps to explain why men are so devastated when a mate dies suddenly.

Men are likely to be task-oriented, their vocation receiving the most emphasis, with relationships second and their own needs last. Little wonder that losing a job is a major catastrophe for them. Society has long demanded that men be vocation-centered.

However, among the generation born in the fifties, that is definitely changing, with self-care rating near the top for both men and women.

Women are likely to be relationship-oriented, with nurture receiving the most emphasis, their own needs next, and vocation last on the list. Small wonder that women still list "being a homemaker" as their first choice, even many women who are employed full-time in well-paying jobs. A job outside the home just doesn't measure up to their image of themselves of care-givers. That, too, is changing among the youth now entering the job and marriage scenes.

The image we have of ourselves determines who we will be. Whoever we envision ourselves to be, that is who we will become.

So many of the terrible things that occur in our world are the result of people disliking themselves so much that they must forever be trying to do something to prove to themselves and to other people that they are important, that they are loved.

The child abuser inevitably turns out to have been abused as a child, for if Mother or Father hated him enough to abuse him,

139

he must deserve their hatred, and he comes to believe that he has no worth. That is the image on which he acts, and every time he abuses his own child, it confirms his belief that he is no good.

The battered wife believes she deserves such treatment. And when I asked my counselor/friend why I had allowed my marriage to deteriorate, she said, "Because you did not love yourself enough to demand more from the marriage. If you had believed you were worth a good marriage, you would have demanded it and helped to make it happen."

A young couple who had been living together for more than five years was having difficulties. Over and over, the man would leave the house for a few hours, a few days, but he would always return to the relationship. Each time he returned, things settled down for a while, but soon she would begin shouting at him again. One time she threw things at him; another time she threatened to do him physical harm if he did not show her the caring she demanded. Still he went back.

Finally one day the young man announced that he was not going back, that he did not deserve to be treated like that. "I allowed her to treat me in a way I would never accept from anyone else. Deep inside of me, I felt guilty, believing I deserved that kind of treatment. Now I know that I am special; I deserve a loving mate."

It is the goal of the Christian faith to persuade every person that God loves them. For if God loves them, they can love themselves; people who love themselves can love other people, and the reign of peace has begun.

Do we have wars because those who continue to build up huge arsenals are, at heart, frightened humans who do not know that God loves them, and must be forever throwing up walls to protect them from those they don't trust? People who trust themselves trust other people.

Again the passage, "Perfect love casts out fear," comes to mind. Fear-determined people are afraid to trust the power of love. Even if it is demonstrated all around them, they cannot believe it is for them, because they do not love themselves.

What makes us understand that we are loved? What brings about that transformation from a frightened, intimidated being to a person who believes she is loved because God loves her?

How many times have you heard the phrase, "God is Love"? How often have you seen "God Loves You" on a sign, on a bumper sticker, in a newsletter? Children are taught from the earliest age to sing "Jesus Loves Me." To understand what that means is to be transformed into loving people, for if God loves us, we are worth loving, because "God don't make no junk."

But what is the entry point of transformation? What is the catalyst that will bring about that moment of truth? If we knew, we could program people to believe they are loved because God loves them, and the churches could go out of the business of conversion. No one can make transformation happen, and no one can keep it from happening.

Transformation is a never-ending process. My own metamorphosis from a person intimidated by a relationship to a person who understands that God loves me is continuing as I discover parts of myself that are still in thrall to something or other. Freedom is not a static condition.

Over and over, I have come out on a plateau and said, "I am free of my bondage to that (relationship, need, hunger.) I didn't even know I was tied to it." We can't get out of a box until we realize we are in a box; we cannot free ourselves until we realize we are in prison; we cannot release our life energies for positive experiences until we quit using them for negative actions.

The moment of transformation comes when we recognize that we are indeed prisoners and set about to free ourselves, something only we can do. No one else can release us from those things that we have allowed to control us, those *shetans* that arise from within ourselves.

Accepting the fact that we will continue to discover ways in which we are in bondage, we can nevertheless begin to understand what self-care looks like.

Chris had worked long hours and some overtime preparing the layout for a brochure. It was the first time she had done it, but not the last, she hoped. The opportunity had appeared suddenly and could mean a step upward.

Moving back to view her work, she congratulated herself for having produced a far better result than the previous person had done.

Suddenly beside her appeared her boss.

"S-a-aay! You did a very good job on that!" he said.

"Thank you," Chris murmured, stumbling, "but it could be better. The printing isn't as clear as it should be, and . . . ."

The boss moved off, and Chris stood looking at her work, feeling vaguely disquieted. Why had she spoken negatively about the layout? There was nothing wrong with the printing; she had made that up. Why?

Chris was no different than many other women. All our lives we have been told not to appear arrogant, especially in relation to a person in authority, and especially to men. The result was that Chris looked less effective than she really felt.

What would have happened if she responded with, "Thank you, I feel good about it too"? A simple acceptance of her achievement. If a person expresses a feeling that she has not measured up, others will accept that assessment. But if she believes she is successful, and shows it, others will believe it too.

As women move into the world outside the home and into the marketplace, they are at a disadvantage. It's hard to succeed in the world of business if your image of yourself is that of putting everyone else first. The other side of that coin is *not* walking over people, but rather developing your own integrity, which becomes the building block for success.

Women give away their power over and over. If you are not succeeding as you would like or as you think you should, perhaps it is because you are not aware that you are giving away your power.

What is meant by power? It is that personal ability to be in charge of your own life, to make things happen for *you*. Only if *you* are in charge and take responsibility for yourself can you expect to succeed.

But the propensity for giving away power is not limited to women. Men are more likely to take the credit for a job well done, but when someone says, "He (a fellow worker) seems like a good guy," a man is likely to say, "I guess so, but he really isn't very good at his job."

Putting down someone else never results in building up yourself. On the contrary, you lose power because the listener wonders what you might say about him in the same situation. It never hurts to say, "He's all right." Praising another person shows that you feel secure about yourself.

There is no better thought to remember than

> *Be kind to one another, tenderhearted,*
> *forgiving one another, as God in Christ forgave you*
>
> EPHESIANS 4:32

An effective way to lose power is to try to take it away from someone else; the best way to acquire power is to empower someone else. What does that look like?

A sincere compliment goes a long way toward making someone feel good about himself. "You did a good job on that display." Emphasis on the "you." It will encourage him to do a good job the next time, thus empowering him.

Only if you have a good feeling about who you are—that is, only if you like yourself—can you have enough power to share it with someone else. In taking power you lose it; by sharing, you increase it. Surely that is what is meant by, "If you would save your life, you must lose it." In being willing to share your power, to give it away, you will find renewed impetus and energy.

But most people, especially women, are afraid of their power. That is due in part to the differing roles for men and women that society allows. Men may exert power; women may not.

My dream about my little Datsun covertible was a dream about power. When I told my counselor about it, the conversation went like this:

C: Close your eyes and tell me the dream just as it happened.

Me: I am driving down the road in my little blue Datsun. Someone tries to run me off the road. Then that person disappears.

C: You are the Datsun. Tell me what it feels like.

Me: Beautiful and powerful and free—most of all, free.

C: No, you are the Datsun. Describe yourself, not the car.

Me: Yes, I know.

C: And you are beautiful, powerful, and free?

Me: Yes.
(He began laughing.)

Me: Why are you laughing?

C: You were telling me just a few minutes ago about how powerless you are and now you describe yourself as beautiful and powerful. Is that what you are?

Me: Yes.

C: Beautiful and powerful and free.

Me: You bet!
(He laughed again.)

C: All right, now you are the person who is trying to run the Datsun off the road.

Me: I thought that was my husband.

C: Usually we are all the people in the dream, disguised. That person is you. Tell me what you are doing.

Me: (I had to think about that.) The Datsun is frightening; I am afraid of it; I must get rid of it.

C: Do you hear yourself saying that you are afraid of that part of you that is the Datsun, your power, and that you need to get rid of it?

Me: Yes. Is that really true, that I am afraid of the Datsun?

C: Yes. That is the part of you that thinks you should not be free and powerful; you are frightened by it. You have let part of you be afraid of your own power and held it back all these years. You must reclaim that power.

The interpretation of that dream did much to help me start reclaiming my belief in myself. But there is another concept that goes along with that.

Using our power means accepting responsibility for making our own decisions. No one else gets the credit when we succeed, and no one can be blamed if something goes wrong. That can be a very lonely place to be, but the satisfaction of being in charge of your life more than makes up for it.

My pastor said, "The only unforgiveable sin is refusing to accept responsibility for our actions." The Old and New Testaments are full of stories of people who did terrible things but were forgiven. To accept responsibility for our actions puts us in charge, for then we are not looking over our shoulder to see who is watching us, fearful that someone will discover *we* did it. To accept the blame, if indeed we deserve it, puts the responsibility squarely on our shoulders, and the power right in our hands. All our energy can be used for the task at hand, not in worrying whether we will be found out.

Is there any more poignant example to illustrate this than the story of David and Bathsheba. After having Bathsheba's husband, Uriah, killed, David took her for his own wife. The prophet, Nathan, made up a beautiful story of a rich man and a poor man. The rich man had many lambs; the poor man had only one little ewe lamb, which lived with him and his children. Nathan waxed emotional and described how the little lamb ate out of the master's plate, drank from his cup, and "lay in his bosom. It was like a daughter to him."

When the rich man had to provide a meal for a visitor in his home, he did not want to use any of his prize lambs, so he took away the poor man's lamb and prepared it for the meal of his guest.

Nathan didn't even get to tell any more of the story before David rose up in righteous anger, shouting, "As the Lord lives, the man who has done this deserves to die!"

In a moment of historic drama, Nathan said to David, "You are the man!"

Unlike Adam and Eve, unlike Jacob, unlike Judas, David owned up to his sinful deed, saying, "I have sinned against the Lord." Since he was the king, he could have dismissed the whole thing, but there was some reason why David became such a great king. It was not because he was so good, but because he was willing to honor his covenant with God.

Even in David's time, Psalm 51 was being sung; he may even have sung it and played it on his harp for King Saul.

The sacrifice acceptable to God is a broken spirit;
a broken and contrite heart, O God, thou wilt not despise.

My son coined a new phrase for people who refuse to believe in themselves; he says they have a "locomotive complex." When faced with a challenge, they say, "I know I can't; I know I can't; I know I can't."

More is required, if you are to adequately provide self-care, than merely refusing to give away your power. Vast amounts of energy are used up in shadow-boxing with people in our lives who have caused us real or imagined hurts. We tell our friend or mate at great lengths what we are "going to" do or say to that person, but most of us lack techniques for handling difficult situations.

When someone has done something so unacceptable that you have to confront him about it, or someone in your daily life is so irritating that you can no longer ignore it, you need a method of dealing with it that will produce the desired result, a change on the part of the other person. It can be called conflict resolution, and although that sounds difficult, there is no mystery about it. There are several elements that should be included in such a confrontation.

146

1. You will want to remain in control; not lose your temper
2. You do not want to just deliver an ultimatum; you want the other person to respond
3. You want to take responsibility for what you are doing

There are four parts to the confrontation:

1. State your feelings, taking responsibility for them
2. Make clear what is the objectionable behavior
3. State what changes you want to see
4. Ask for a response

It might go something like this: "I feel irritated when you always arrive late for our meetings. From now on I want you to either arrive on time or let me know in advance. How do you feel about that?"

You have accepted responsibility by saying "I." The use of "you" is always a red flag, signaling an accusation. You have explained what emotion is aroused by saying, "I feel irritated," or angry, or whatever. You have made clear what action would be acceptable, but you also give them a chance to respond. You are not just dumping your frustration on them.

Those living together in a household could benefit from such a technique, for in so doing, you can,

Let each of you look not only to his own interests,
but also to the interests of others.

PHILIPPIANS 2:4

The Bible tell us that

God emptied himself, taking the form of a servant.

PHILIPPIANS 2:7

Taking the initiative to handle family annoyances is the servant role that could mean significant changes in relationships in your family.

Picking up after the children neither teaches them to be responsible nor gives Mother a feeling of self-respect. So Mother might say, "I feel angry when you drop your wet towel in a heap on the floor of the bathroom. I want you to hang it on the rack where it belongs. How do you feel about that?"

If you do not take care of some of the little irritations in your daily experience, they will eat away at you, draining your energy. Confronting them and resolving them will free that energy.

Taking care of yourself will include a number of the concepts already discussed in this book—sharing your pain, discovering your "Other"; setting your own goals; learning how to heal yourself; learning what is sacred within you. All those are positives.

But there may be relationships in your life that, at this moment, are strictly toxic. Until something creative can be done about resolving the problems between you, you must somehow live with that person in your world. What can you do to protect yourself from excessive pain and trauma?

Sometimes walls are an excellent form of self-care. If you need a wall between you and another person, build it carefully, for walls keep you in as well as the other person out.

The wall could be built by placing layer upon layer of negative things about the other person. It would probably be effective in protecting you, but maintaining that wall will require considerable energy, and it will be an ugly wall. After a while, people looking at you might see the ugly wall instead of you.

Try using building blocks that are all the good things about you. This is known as an Integrity Wall. No one can breach that parapet, for surrounding yourself with your good qualities will turn your energies from negative to positive. The people around you will sense positive vibrations coming from you.

If there is a particularly toxic person in your life, put her in a box. Envision it in your mind; she is in a box, and she may come out only with your permission. Even as you are speaking with her, imagine her in a box. With a little practice you will find that you can deal with that person as you have to, and as soon as the interview is over, you replace the lid on the box and leave that relationship until something creative can be done about it. You will not be throwing away energy on something that is futile, and you will feel that you are in charge, a necessary ingredient to dispel fear.

Another method is to change the person's name. Choose a name and use only that reference when thinking or speaking of that person. Changing the name will alter the image, which will in turn begin to eliminate some of the poisons that have been built up over the years in that relationship, so that they are not factors in present decisions.

Remember, words have the power to provide alternative models. Change the words, and you can discover different patterns of behavior.

Taking care of yourself first will mean that you nurture the relationships around you and discover the vocation that is best suited for you, building it all on the knowledge that God loves you.

In the book of Matthew, the master said to the servant who had used his talents well, "Well done, good and faithful servant; you have been faithful over a little, I will set you over much; enter into the joy of your master."

"I wish I were twenty years younger," I said.

My son said, "What if you were twenty years older; then you could wish you were twenty years younger." I stared at him. He was right! I wouldn't want to be twenty years older, and, in fact, I wouldn't want to be twenty years younger. Wanting to be who you are at this very moment is power, for you aren't wasting energy dreaming about who you might be or what you might accomplish, if only . . .

Instead, you are using the gifts you know are your very own, your unique contribution to the world, and you are able to do this because you understand that self-care is not selfish; it is accepting that God loves you and is absolutely essential to your becoming the person you are envisioning. When you know who you are and are glad to be who you are, then you can reach out to others without fear or reservation, and you are both empowered and enriched.

chapter eighteen

Renewed Energy Through Faith

Never in the history of America have so many people been so interested in energy, particularly our own body energy. We jog, exercise, meditate, watch our diets, eat special foods, all to build up our bodies so that we have available the energy we want and need.

But all the body-building foods and activities in the world cannot provide the energy we need if our soul-building is neglected.

The question is, "What is the source of the energy that allows me to continue the life-direction that I have chosen?"

There could be several answers to that question:

The energy comes from

† my work, when I see that paycheck
† my friends, when they respond to my friendship needs

† my family, when they give me respect and support

† my church, when it gives me a sense of belonging

† God, when He answers my prayers

† my spouse, when he/she responds in caring ways

But each of those answers is outside of ourselves. Over and over in this book we have discussed the idea that first, we accept God's love. Then we can understand that *we* are responsible for our lives; *we* are the ones who determine whether we will be happy; *we* are the ones who must decide whether to reach out, to share our pain, to look after ourselves.

The energy necessary for such victorious living, initiated by our faith, flows into our beings from the Source of Power to which we are tied, and then moves out into the lives of others.

In the play *Children of the Promise*, John had spent centuries seeking the Source in someone else but never finding it. The other people were always inadequate, less than acceptable, sinners. When, through a loving relationship with Amanda, his wife, he came to realize the the Promise was within him, he suddenly began to see it in other people. He changed from a suspicious, frightened, muscle-bound man, unable to reach out to others, to a hopeful, happy, energetic person who could care about those whom only a short time before he had written off as inadequate.

Living our lives through others; forever waiting for someone else to make good things happen for us; blaming God or other people when things don't go our way; being afraid of the powerful people in our lives—in all of these ways we refuse to reach out and take the Power that is ours. Not only do we refuse the Power, we use up vital energy being afraid, angry, or frustrated.

The promises are there in Isaiah 40:29, "He gives power to the faint, and to them that have no might, he increases strength."

But these are frightening times! How can we have faith when our world is in such a mess? Sometimes it seems to be falling apart.

Ilya Prigogine, a Belgian chemist, won the 1977 Nobel Prize by addressing this idea.

His theory says that everything alive is surprisingly alive—and on a twitchy, searching, self-aware, self-organizing, upward journey. Such living systems periodically break into *severe* twitchiness and appear to fall apart. They aren't. It is actually at such vibrating times that living systems (humans, chemical solutions, whole societies) are shaking themselves to higher ground.

Prigogine has further advanced the startling idea (first gathered from observations of complex chemical solutions) that *transition* to a higher order is *universally* accompanied by turbulence or, to use Prigogine's word, 'perturbation.' He says that the disorder and disharmony in any chemical solution (or any society?) is a *necessary* activation of growth to a higher level. Prigogine sees the familiar evidence of decline as the actual harbinger and stimulant of change to a higher order!

What he is saying is this: living things, always unstable even in good times, will occasionally go into extreme fluctuation and perturbation and appear to be falling apart. Take heart: this is an even *better* time! The apparent disharmony is the way that every living thing re-jiggles itself into new combinations and permutations for ever-higher, ever-newer levels of development.[15]

Another way of saying that is the Hebrew writer's words, *"There come times when God takes the world and He shakes it so as to reveal the things that cannot be shaken."*

There were numerous times in the past four years when I knew my world was falling apart, for, look, it was shaking, obviously in great turmoil and trouble. Only now I know that I was being shaken into a higher level of understanding.

This concept came to me two years ago, and one would think that I would have been able, from then on, to walk serenely through the times of soul-shaking experiences, knowing that God was in charge of the "shattering and blinding white light" that surrounded me. But over and over I was dragged, kicking and screaming, into the Valley of the Shadow. Even though I *knew* (intellectually) that death was the prelude to New Life, and that resurrection followed death; nevertheless, my being went, trembling and terrified, to God to ask what in "Hell" was going on.

The most terrifying time of all came when my name was taken away, and I became "Nobody."

John had moved out, and that July day he was coming back so we could divide our possessions, those collected items of shared experiences. The stereo records, the mementoes from travels, the rocking chairs . . .

We moved through the house, tense and terse, keeping the conversation strictly on an arms-length basis. He had made that footstool in high school—it should be his, of course. That old book belonged to his Uncle Wayne, that cream pitcher to his mother. And the piano, originally a gift from his parents, would go to Ellen, our daughter. I had spent many pleasant hours playing the piano, but . . .

In "our" bedroom I stood looking at the beautiful handmade dresser, crafted in 1856 for another Mrs. Allen, John's great grandmother. Sometimes when I dusted it, I had felt close to that other Mrs. Allen in whose name and lineage I followed. But, of course, the dresser would stay in the family; anything that had come from John's family would stay with him.

Thirty-three years of marriage and nothing belonged to me. Suddenly I couldn't go on. "Let's do this another time," I said. "I . . . it's much too hot right now."

He left very soon.

I dropped into the big arm chair in the front room and let my feelings wash over me. As I had done since the beginning of this experience, some months before, I allowed myself to be submerged in the feelings, the emotion of the moment. Fear, anger, pain—all of them. I had discovered that by immersing myself in them, they passed more quickly, and by not denying the deepest level of feeling, I could take from it the gift of learning.

I did that then, letting the thoughts flow without any attempt to organize or impede them.

Talking aloud seemed to help me think.

"For thirty-three years I have been on loan from the Maguire family to the Allen family. I have given birth to four children with the name of Allen.

"John does not want to continue the relationship. I have been Mrs. John Allen for thirty-three years. As of the time John moved out, Mrs. John Allen ceased to exist, for he took that name with him. But I *was* Mrs. John Allen for thirty-three years. If Mrs. John Allen does not exist, then I don't exist!

"I can't go back to being Maguire—that was too long ago. I gave up my family thirty-three years ago to become Allen.

"At this moment I have no name . . . no family . . . no roots . . . no financial base of security . . . no emotional support system that comes from family. I have no past and therefore no future, because the future comes out of the past.

"And so, at this moment, I am nobody! *Nobody!*"

I gave myself to my tears and felt swept into the terrible darkness of nothingness, of being *nobody*.

Driving alone in the car is the very best time for me to look deeply inside myself, uninterrupted. The next morning I was driving to my friend's house for the weekend, a nine-hour drive. A few times during this life accident I went beyond anger to rage. This was one of them.

To make matters worse, in the pre-dawn preparations, I stumbled against a chair, striking one of my little toes, and, I learned later, breaking it. My already anguished tears were multiplied.

Anger is the feeling you have when someone does something to upset you. Often anger is really disgust at ourselves for letting someone control us or for not being as strong as we might be. Rage is different. It is anger at something you can't do anything about.

Thirty-three years before, society had required that I give up my name and family and devote my entire life to John Allen. I could not have refused to do that, given the context of society in those times. Now society was saying that it was all right for him to take away my name!

And so I raged!

Over and over I cried aloud, my voice soon becoming hoarse. "If I am no longer the person I have been for thirty-three years, then who am I?

"Mrs. Dorris Allen? Dorris Maguire Allen? Dorris Allen Maguire?

"To what name shall I answer? To what name shall I respond?

"I am a writer. In whose name shall I write? In the name of Dorris Maguire? In the name of Dorris Allen? In the name of Jesus Christ!"

Abruptly my tears stopped. ". . . In the name of Jesus Christ," I said again.

And suddenly I knew the answer, the answer to who I was. And, for the first time in my fifty-four years, I knew why the Christian says, ". . . in the name of Jesus Christ."

Again I spoke, but now with a strong voice. "There comes a time when, because of broken relationships, we discover that we are 'nobody'; we have no identity, no name of our own, and in our lostness and our aloneness we discover that to do something in the name of Jesus Christ is to take on the name and image of Christ."

The image of Christ was very real to me, for had I not met Him in my "desert"; had He not been my refuge and strength in the Darkness?

Again I spoke aloud. "I now have my own separate identity and personhood. I am Jean Christ!"

I wept again, copious tears, but now of joy. I had a name, my own special, unique name, one that no one on this earth, nor death—no, not even death—could take away!

And I knew at that moment that I was not afraid to die, but more important, I was not afraid to live. For I was no longer "Nobody!"

The rest of the journey was a joyous one as I explored with equal excitement who the new person that I now was could become.

Later a friend, hearing my story, gave me a gift of a scripture passage from Revelation 2:17, "To her that overcometh will I give a white stone, and in the stone a new name written, which no one knoweth save she who receiveth it."

"The Bible is a living book!" I exclaimed. "Look! It writes about me! And about anyone else who loses their name and finds their real one."

That time, as each time in the past, I emerged from wrestling with my Angel, exhausted but triumphant, with yet another scar to indicate that I had indeed been touched by God. The crooked little toe on my left foot reminds me of how I wrestled with my angel, and won.

How can you understand how very important you are to God?

God had an idea, one he wanted humans to understand, an idea that was around from the beginning of time. God wanted us to know the most basic, the most important truth of all time.

He kept trying to get through to the Children of Israel. Years before the coming of the Christ Child, Isaiah said,

> *Unto us a child is born,*
> *unto us a son is given,*
> *and the government shall be upon his shoulders*
> *and his name shall be Wonderful Counselor,*
> *the Mighty God, the Prince of Peace.*

But Isaiah was not a seer envisioning an old man and a young woman trudging reluctantly to Bethlehem seven hundred years later. His message was that it is through the birth of humans that hope comes into the world.

Many years later God demonstrated that truth; Jesus, the Christ, was born.

If we see that baby being born and think that is the truth of all time, we are blinded from the truth by the truth.

We should not mistake the importance of that event; the Son of God was born, the Christ became human.

But God was trying to tell us a far more important truth, and that was:

"History is open, and the vehicle by which the divine opens history eternally is the human womb, which is us."[16]

Each time the womb is opened and a child is born, hope is renewed. That is why each child is precious, because through the birth of each person, there is hope.

Can that be true? Are all those people, all those babies being born, important? Each one of us was one of those babies being born. Are *we* that important?

. Do we dare believe that?

Do we dare *not* believe that?

Hear it another way.

Because *you* were born, there is hope.

So many of us do not know this most important of all truths. We keep asking, "Why was I born upon this earth?" And we come up with answers, but we don't listen for God's answer.

But God is patient.

Hear the answer! The moment of our own salvation comes when we realize that truth and hope are reborn on the earth in a moment of mystery and great joy, when you and I affirm the meaning of our birth. At that moment we are reborn.

When you were born, the Son of God, the Daughter of God, was born.

When you were born, Christ came again to earth.

God is alive, not just because it says so in the Bible, although it does.

God is alive because *you* are alive!

Frightening!

It lays the burden on me and you!

Empowering!

It places the joy of new life in my hands and yours.

There is hope! *We* are that hope!

My part in the salvation of the world is not the same as yours, and yours is not like mine; but yours is as important as mine, and mine is as significant as yours.

In a moment of mystery—and maybe some fear, but a moment of joy—let us relive our birth, let us be born again.

Let the Spirit speak to you, through you, as you say:

"Because I, _____ , was born, salvation has come.

"Because I, _____ , was born, there is hope for the world."

That is the truth of the ages!

There is no point in wondering why in the world God would keep coming back to us when we never seem to learn our lesson. Merely accept the mystery of the Grace of God, and keep asking God to, "Tell me one more time that I'm all right; that, yes, you love me."

And every time, God will!

And you will feel again the strength you need to pull on your tether and move yet farther out.

Thus is faith reconfirmed and energy renewed!

Notes

1. Walter Brueggemann, "We Meet God in the Darkness" (Speech delivered to the Church of the Brethren Annual Conference, Indianapolis, June 1981).

2. Ibid.

3. Henri Nouwen, *The Wounded Healer* (New York: Doubleday & Co., 1972) p. 84.

4. Ada Jackson, "To Judas Iscariot."

5. Henri Nouwen, "The Spirituality of the Desert," in *Sojourners* (Washington, D.C.: People's Christian Coalition, June, 1980) p. 14.

6. John Harris, *Stress, Power, and Ministry* (Washington, D.C.: Alban Institute, 1980) p. 39.

7. Rollo May, *Love and Will* (New York: W.W. Norton Co., 1969) p. 151.

8. Robert G. Statler Mock, "When Sickness Comes" (Nampa, Idaho: Church of the Brethren, 1981).

9. Ibid.

10. Ted A. Grossbat, "Bringing Peace to Embattled Skin," in *Psychology Today* (New York: February, 1982).

11. Marilyn Ferguson, *Aquarian Conspiracy* (Los Angeles, CA: J.P. Tarcher, Inc., 1980) p. 76.

12. Gail Sheehy, *Pathfinders* (New York: William Morrow & Co., Inc., 1981) p. 77.

13. Brueggemann, "We Meet God in the Darkness."

14. Henri Nouwen, *Clowning in Rome* (Garden City, N.Y.: Image Books, Doubleday & Co., Inc., 1979) pp. 46-50.

15. Robert L. Schwartz, "Scientific Theories," in *Tarrytown Newsletter* (Tarrytown, N.Y.: March, 1982).

16. Herbert O'Driscoll, "Changing Ministry" (Speech delivered to the Consultation on the Future of Ministry, Toronto, Canada, 1980).